Complete Horoscope

Libra 2022

Monthly astrological forecasts for 2022

TATIANA BORSCH

Translated from Russian by Sonja Swenson-Khalchenia
Translation copyright © Coinflow Limited, Cyprus
AstraArt Books is an imprint of Coinflow limited, Cyprus
Published by Coinflow Limited, Cyprus
For queries please contact: tatianaborsch@yahoo.com

ISBN: 978-9925-579-68-6 (print)
ISBN: 978-9925-579-69-3 (ebook)

Contents

2022 – A World Still in Flux

We survived the incredible stress of 2020-2021, when our world's very foundation seemed to be falling apart under us. What does 2022 have in store?

According to the stars, the coming year can be divided into two distinct periods: a very favorable time during the first half of the year, and trouble during the second half.

Politics and Economy

From January to July, things will be serene and predictable.

Jupiter and Neptune will dominate this period, and nearly all year long, they will have very strong energy in Pisces. Jupiter's contact with other planets, including Uranus and Pluto, will be exceptionally favorable during the first half of 2022, so we can count on calm, steady waters...

Together in Pisces, Jupiter and Neptune rule the areas of medicine, oil, space, and the sea. Their favorable aspects mean that this is where we can expect a lot of developments in 2022. In addition to medicine, oil, and space, Jupiter and Neptune also rule the arts, so we can expect incredible feats in film, music, and painting. Many of these pieces will have a space or maritime theme.

Neptune also rules everything related to drugs and alcohol, and 2022 may bring a trend toward legalizing drugs in many countries. This will mainly include "soft" drugs, such as marijuana. This is also a promising time for the wine industry, and Jupiter's powerful influence means that we might see increasing production, and more public attention on elite, luxury wine brands.

For now, we will still have to deal with problems related to the economy, but during the first half of the year, they will likely be somewhat mitigated and under control. One way or another the world will start to shake off the coronavirus epidemic, with help from vaccines and new, effective treatments.

Many countries, including Russia, the United States, and China, will rebuild their economies, and shift their direction and approach. Here, we can consider China as the unrefuted global leader.

During the first half of the year, we might see cryptocurrencies experience serious growth, along with the emergence of new cryptocurrencies.

Things are looking less sunny for the EU countries. Despite the fact that the interminable lockdowns will finally come to an end, economies will continue to struggle, and political clashes will continue.

However, during the first half of the year, from January until mid-August, these negative trends will be somewhat less noticeable.

Things in the United States are looking much more peaceful, though Republicans will become more powerful and influential in 2022.

During the first half of the year, the political horizon of our turbulent world is looking relatively quiet. There will be a trend toward resalable relationships toward war and peace, and there may even be major agreements between countries, which will be largely responsible for this state of affairs.

Beginning in the second half of August 2022, however, things will suddenly take a dark turn. Confrontation from Mars is the theme of the second half of the year. This will lead to negativity, crises, and war. In May 2022, Jupiter will also shift from neutral Pisces to belligerent Aries.

The international stage will once again become difficult, and many countries will fail to shoulder their agreements, with hotspots popping up all over the globe. This may become extremely challenging, as Uranus, an abrupt planet full of the unexpected, will be in the same degree of Taurus that it was in 1938, which was a fateful year for the entire world.

Remember that 1938 was the year that Germany, Poland, and Romania divided Czechoslovakia with the agreement of England and France. From an astrological point of view, this is the event that triggered World War Two. Of course, astrology is not alone here – when describing the dissolution of Czechoslovakia, Winston Churchill himself stated that "England has been offered a choice between war and shame. She has chosen shame, and will get war."

Uranus has an 84-year cycle. Its passage through Taurus has always brought large-scale war, including in 1853-1856, with the Crimean Wars, between the Russian Empire and a coalition made up of Britain, France, the Ottoman Empire, and Sardinia.

Uranus entered Taurus on May 5, 2018, and will remain there until April 26, 2026. We already know that between 2018 and 2021, military tensions have escalated around the world. Unfortunately, this is only the beginning of what may continue for a long time into the future.

Warmongering rhetoric and possibly even clashes in hotspots will be more common during the second half of the year, but this will result in the weakening of NATO countries, with China and Russia growing stronger. This may continue into 2023-2024.

During this time, many countries will experience spontaneous protests and unrest. People will begin to resist authority much more strongly, which will force authorities to make some concessions and adopt certain measures, as many countries will find themselves moving closer to revolution. Countries suffering from economic instability are likely to see changes in government, if not outright political chaos.

The horoscope for the United States indicates that in the second half of 2022, there will be turbulence as well as the revelation of certain secrets. Former President Donald Trump will take on an active role and should not be written off. His influence on US citizens will only grow, but political positions will in general become more hardline. All of that will go along with a serious struggle and clashes with democratic institutions.

Protests and unrest are to be expected in Russia, too, during this time. However, President Putin will hold onto power, though there may be some changes to various government bodies. The changes that began with changes in government in 2020 may continue. Of course, some people will suffer, but overall, this will be a good thing for society.

The economic and political situation in Ukraine may worsen in the long term. Military activity in the eastern territories of Luhansk and Donetsk will continue, and that may end poorly for Kyiv, and it will become clear that these territories will never be returned to Ukraine.

Problems that arise during the second half of 2022 will continue during the three months of 2023.

Climate

The climate will continue to change. Jupiter and Neptune will bring major floods that are worse than what we have seen in the last several years. People living in coastal areas should consider this and take the utmost precautions when preparing for spring. Volcanos will also become more active. Glaciers will continue melting, and there is nothing we can do to halt this process.

In late May, Jupiter will move into fiery Aries, and remain there until the end of October. This means that during this time, we can expect fires to break out around the world, causing major ecological and human losses.

In seismically active zones, we can expect major earthquakes.

Health

In 2022, we may see new, unique treatments for serious illnesses such as diabetes and cancer.

From May to November, people should be very careful if they suffer from heart disease or various allergies. In the fall and winter of 2022, we might see new outbreaks of respiratory infections.

During the second half of 2022, we might also see the emergence of new types of diseases. We may also learn new information about the manmade origins of coronavirus, which dominated our world in 2020 and 2021.

Personal Life

The first half of 2022 is a good time for buying real estate or opening up a business.

Single people might meet someone special, and Pisces, those born in the first ten days of Aries, as well as Virgo and Capricorn will be ahead of the rest of the planet in this regard.

Any marriages that take place between January and May are sure to be stable and happy.

Children born in 2022 might grow up to be talented musicians, highly creative, and have extrasensory abilities. In time, they will become inspiring leaders who will steer the world to a positive place.

During the fall and winter of 2022, things will be rocker in politics as well as personal relations. Many people will reconsider their links to others, and a real crisis or breakdown is likely.

If that is your case, remember that any crisis and break with the past is the key to true change, new opportunities, and a new life! This is the only way we can deal with the twists and turns Fate throws our way!

2022 Overview for Libra

2022 will be a hard year full of selfless labor. This is not a burden, per se, and is in fact a continuation of the path you have been on for some time. But keep moving forward, and don't forget to look behind you every now and then. You need to watch your back!

Work. Overall, 2022 is a positive time for you. During the first half, you will advance and achieve stable professional growth. Entrepreneurs will continue developing their business, which they began in the fall of 2021, and by the summer of 2022, they will have reached a new level, with commensurate profits.

Employees can expect incredible career opportunities, either right where they are or at a new, more promising company. You might have additional responsibilities which will improve your professional and financial situation.

Starting in September, however, what seemed like a stable situation will unexpectedly start to waver. You might expect audits, which will cause you to doubt everything you have recently achieved. Unflattering information may be released, which will seriously harm your reputation. This is the case for both employees and entrepreneurs.

Employees might even be fired over the revelations.

Alternatively, partners in other cities or abroad may behave aggressively, and their erratic behavior will cause a breakdown in your relationship as well as major business losses.

Remember this during the first, favorable half of the year, especially if you work with colleagues who are far away. The problems may become very serious, and are likely to drag on until December.

Money. During the first half of 2022, your income will be noticeably stable, especially in late February, March, the second half of June and July. During the second half of the year, in late October and November, things will also look decent.

Love and family. Your personal and romantic life might look less noteworthy than work and the litany of tasks taking up all of your time.

In late May, June, and July, you can count on meeting people and possibly a romance, which will continue until the fall. It is impossible to predict what will happen during the difficult fall months, but many families will face problems involving relatives – likely your in-laws or the family of your most recent fling.

This may lead to arguments or issues with a close relative.

The stars recommend carefully examining all potential outcomes and laying the groundwork as soon as possible so that you are not caught off guard.

Health. In 2022, many Libras will quit their bad habits and finally take their health seriously. The stars urge you to get some exercise, follow a healthy diet, and practice regular self-care.

From September to December, be careful when traveling and driving – there is a high likelihood of traffic accidents.

January

New York Time				London Time		
Calendar Day	Lunar Day	Lunar Day Start Time		Calendar Day	Lunar Day	Lunar Day Start Time
01/01/2022	29	6:06 AM		01/01/2022	29	6:42 AM
02/01/2022	30	7:10 AM		02/01/2022	30	7:49 AM
02/01/2022	1	1:35 PM		02/01/2022	1	6:35 PM
03/01/2022	2	8:06 AM		03/01/2022	2	8:42 AM
04/01/2022	3	8:51 AM		04/01/2022	3	9:21 AM
05/01/2022	4	9:29 AM		05/01/2022	4	9:51 AM
06/01/2022	5	10:01 AM		06/01/2022	5	10:15 AM
07/01/2022	6	10:30 AM		07/01/2022	6	10:36 AM
08/01/2022	7	10:56 AM		08/01/2022	7	10:54 AM
09/01/2022	8	11:23 AM		09/01/2022	8	11:12 AM
10/01/2022	9	11:49 AM		10/01/2022	9	11:30 AM
11/01/2022	10	12:18 PM		11/01/2022	10	11:51 AM
12/01/2022	11	12:50 PM		12/01/2022	11	12:15 PM
13/01/2022	12	1:27 PM		13/01/2022	12	12:44 PM
14/01/2022	13	2:08 PM		14/01/2022	13	1:20 PM
15/01/2022	14	2:56 PM		15/01/2022	14	2:05 PM
16/01/2022	15	3:49 PM		16/01/2022	15	2:58 PM
17/01/2022	16	4:46 PM		17/01/2022	16	3:58 PM
18/01/2022	17	5:47 PM		18/01/2022	17	5:05 PM
19/01/2022	18	6:49 PM		19/01/2022	18	6:15 PM
20/01/2022	19	7:52 PM		20/01/2022	19	7:26 PM
21/01/2022	20	8:56 PM		21/01/2022	20	8:38 PM
22/01/2022	21	10:00 PM		22/01/2022	21	9:52 PM
23/01/2022	22	11:06 PM		23/01/2022	22	11:06 PM
25/01/2022	23	12:14 AM		25/01/2022	23	12:23 AM
26/01/2022	24	1:24 AM		26/01/2022	24	1:42 AM
27/01/2022	25	2:35 AM		27/01/2022	25	3:02 AM
28/01/2022	26	3:45 AM		28/01/2022	26	4:19 AM
29/01/2022	27	4:51 AM		29/01/2022	27	5:30 AM
30/01/2022	28	5:50 AM		30/01/2022	28	6:28 AM
31/01/2022	29	6:40 AM		31/01/2022	29	7:13 AM

You can find the description of each lunar day in the chapter "A Guide to The Moon Cycle and Lunar Days"

The first month of the year is a time for you to sit back and take stock of the past year. You are beginning a new stage, and it's best to get ready in a calm, family environment.

Work. During the first half of the month, work is quiet. From the outside, it might look as though nothing is happening, but it's just the calm before the storm. You might not notice, but work is taking you on a path toward career growth.

Nothing will happen before the second half of February, or even March, but right now, in January, there is nothing stopping you from pondering and discussing the advantages and disadvantages with your loved ones and inner circle.

If you give yourself some time away, then the stars will ensure that things continue moving without you.

Your ties to colleagues in other cities or abroad will move along with varying success. Some things will work out, and others will not. Just like anything.

Business owners might be immersed in organizational tasks, and likely to be dealing with various concerns related to real estate.

Money. January is likely to be modest, financially. Both expenses and income are predictable, moderate, and reasonable this month. You can expect to receive money on January 16, 17, 25, and 26. In addition to your own money, expect help from a family member.

Love and family. For most Libras, January, particularly the first two weeks, is a long-awaited opportunity to spend time with your family and loved ones, and no matter where you to prefer to spend the holiday season – at the beach, on the couch, or in the countryside, you are sure to find love and care with those you love.

The second half of January will involve spending time taking care of your children, and once again, they are going to require a large share of the family budget.

Many Libras will deal with issues related to real estate. You might have to do some minor repairs, or major constructions, or something similar.

Couples will face stormy waters during the second half of the month. During this time, you can expect disagreements, a lot of back-and-forth, and uncertainty about yourself as well as your better half.

You may find yourself having to go back in time to revive still-simmering relationships that are ready to erupt with new vigor. In theory, you are trying to put an end to this love story – after all, it brings you nothing but trouble, and in general, nothing is going right. But that is unlikely to actually happen...

Health. It seems you have been between a rock and a hard place for a while now, and you're tired of it. Remember, exhaustion leads to illness. The prescription is easy – just rest, and then rest again! January is the perfect time for it!

February

New York Time			London Time		
Calendar Day	Lunar Day	Lunar Day Start Time	Calendar Day	Lunar Day	Lunar Day Start Time
01/02/2022	1	12:49 AM	01/02/2022	1	5:49 AM
01/02/2022	2	7:22 AM	01/02/2022	2	7:48 AM
02/02/2022	3	7:57 AM	02/02/2022	3	8:15 AM
03/02/2022	4	8:28 AM	03/02/2022	4	8:38 AM
04/02/2022	5	8:56 AM	04/02/2022	5	8:57 AM
05/02/2022	6	9:23 AM	05/02/2022	6	9:16 AM
06/02/2022	7	9:50 AM	06/02/2022	7	9:35 AM
07/02/2022	8	10:19 AM	07/02/2022	8	9:55 AM
08/02/2022	9	10:50 AM	08/02/2022	9	10:18 AM
09/02/2022	10	11:25 AM	09/02/2022	10	10:45 AM
10/02/2022	11	12:04 PM	10/02/2022	11	11:18 AM
11/02/2022	12	12:50 PM	11/02/2022	12	11:59 AM
12/02/2022	13	1:40 PM	12/02/2022	13	12:49 PM
13/02/2022	14	2:36 PM	13/02/2022	14	1:47 PM
14/02/2022	15	3:36 PM	14/02/2022	15	2:52 PM
15/02/2022	16	4:38 PM	15/02/2022	16	4:01 PM
16/02/2022	17	5:42 PM	16/02/2022	17	5:13 PM
17/02/2022	18	6:47 PM	17/02/2022	18	6:26 PM
18/02/2022	19	7:52 PM	18/02/2022	19	7:40 PM
19/02/2022	20	8:58 PM	19/02/2022	20	8:56 PM
20/02/2022	21	10:06 PM	20/02/2022	21	10:12 PM
21/02/2022	22	11:15 PM	21/02/2022	22	11:31 PM
23/02/2022	23	12:25 AM	23/02/2022	23	12:50 AM
24/02/2022	24	1:34 AM	24/02/2022	24	2:07 AM
25/02/2022	25	2:40 AM	25/02/2022	25	3:18 AM
26/02/2022	26	3:40 AM	26/02/2022	26	4:19 AM
27/02/2022	27	4:31 AM	27/02/2022	27	5:08 AM
28/02/2022	28	5:15 AM	28/02/2022	28	5:45 AM

You can find the description of each lunar day in the chapter "A Guide to The Moon Cycle and Lunar Days"

You are moving forward in leaps and bounds, but the competition is breathing down your neck, trying to steal your place in the sun. Don't let your guard down, keep moving, and do whatever you think you have to.

Work. In February, you will be preoccupied with organizational and other logistical duties. You might be expanding your business, or be working on various real estate transactions. This time, everything you planned will go off smoothly, without a hitch, which will become much clearer toward the middle of the month.

Expanding your business might require new skills, and new, more skilled assistants. Responsible entrepreneurs and demanding bosses will be looking to recruit someone, and closer to the end of the month, they will find their diamond in the rough. You will find the right people, and this will reflect positively on your business.

Employees might be given additional responsibilities, and the stars see this as something very promising. In some cases, you may even be promoted or receive a raise.

Money. Your finances are looking stable this month. In addition to your usual income, you can count on something extra, possibly from a real estate transaction. You can expect credit on beneficial terms, or financial support from a business partner.

Those who are not part of the business world can expect support from parents, a loved one, or their spouse.

Love and family. In many cases, most of your attention will be focused at home and on your family. You are facing difficult issues related to real estate. You might be continuing major construction, restoration, or purchasing a house, apartment, or summer house. That might be for your own family's needs, or for one of your children.

You can expect a lot of hassle and expense, but things will work out in your favor. You will be able to handle the task at hand.

Couples might channel their desire for home improvement, which will only bring them closer together. Romance is very sexy and all, but your day-to-day concerns aren't going away.

Health. You are beginning a long period in which you will need to take your health very seriously. Your diet, a healthy lifestyle, and getting enough sleep are the key to taking care of your body and mind. You need to find an inner balance right now in order to achieve stability, both at work and in your relationships.

March

New York Time			London Time		
Calendar Day	Lunar Day	Lunar Day Start Time	Calendar Day	Lunar Day	Lunar Day Start Time
01/03/2022	29	5:53 AM	01/03/2022	29	6:15 AM
02/03/2022	30	6:25 AM	02/03/2022	30	6:39 AM
02/03/2022	1	12:38 PM	02/03/2022	1	5:38 PM
03/03/2022	2	6:54 AM	03/03/2022	2	7:00 AM
04/03/2022	3	7:22 AM	04/03/2022	3	7:19 AM
05/03/2022	4	7:49 AM	05/03/2022	4	7:38 AM
06/03/2022	5	8:18 AM	06/03/2022	5	7:57 AM
07/03/2022	6	8:48 AM	07/03/2022	6	8:19 AM
08/03/2022	7	9:22 AM	08/03/2022	7	8:45 AM
09/03/2022	8	10:00 AM	09/03/2022	8	9:16 AM
10/03/2022	9	10:43 AM	10/03/2022	9	9:54 AM
11/03/2022	10	11:31 AM	11/03/2022	10	10:40 AM
12/03/2022	11	12:25 PM	12/03/2022	11	11:34 AM
13/03/2022	12	1:23 PM	13/03/2022	12	12:36 PM
14/03/2022	13	2:24 PM	14/03/2022	13	1:44 PM
15/03/2022	14	3:27 PM	15/03/2022	14	2:55 PM
16/03/2022	15	4:32 PM	16/03/2022	15	4:08 PM
17/03/2022	16	5:38 PM	17/03/2022	16	5:23 PM
18/03/2022	17	6:45 PM	18/03/2022	17	6:39 PM
19/03/2022	18	7:54 PM	19/03/2022	18	7:57 PM
20/03/2022	19	9:05 PM	20/03/2022	19	9:17 PM
21/03/2022	20	10:16 PM	21/03/2022	20	10:37 PM
22/03/2022	21	11:26 PM	22/03/2022	21	11:57 PM
24/03/2022	22	12:34 AM	24/03/2022	22	1:10 AM
25/03/2022	23	1:35 AM	25/03/2022	23	2:14 AM
26/03/2022	24	2:28 AM	26/03/2022	24	3:06 AM
27/03/2022	25	3:13 AM	27/03/2022	25	4:46 AM
28/03/2022	26	3:52 AM	28/03/2022	26	5:17 AM
29/03/2022	27	4:25 AM	29/03/2022	27	5:42 AM
30/03/2022	28	4:54 AM	30/03/2022	28	6:04 AM
31/03/2022	29	5:22 AM	31/03/2022	29	6:23 AM

You can find the description of each lunar day in the chapter "A Guide to The Moon Cycle and Lunar Days"

This month your hard work and dedication is a thing to envy. You will succeed wherever you go, be everywhere, and excel at whatever task you take on. Just how do you do it? ☺

Work. You'll have a lot of work on your plate this month, and most of it will be administrative in nature. Entrepreneurs and managers will be checking on their subordinates, and maybe changing up their staffing. You may see new employees arrive, and they will provide much needed and highly valued assistance.

Employees may be given additional responsibilities and a nice bonus to go with. There may even be a promotion and raise on the horizon.

Overall, you're on an active, productive streak, and the stars recommend you remember that the more original and out-of-the-box your ideas are, the more successful they will be.

Money. In March, money is at the very forefront, and you can expect to see a lot of success here. You will have regular income and a lot more than usual. In addition to your usual salary, you can also count on additional profits, either from a bonus, raise, or support from your business partners, or loved ones.

You might even receive some nice dividends from banking transactions or a beneficial loan.

Expect to receive the largest sums on March 2, 3, 11, 12, 21, 22, 29-31.

Love and family. For much of March, you will be focused on work, and you might not have much time left over for your personal life. But just as before, many Libras will find themselves paying more attention and money to their children. You are facing regular expenses related to your children, and the stars recommend that you analyze the situation carefully – do your children really need such largesse? If they do, then there is nothing else to say, but if there is any doubt, think things over again before getting your wallet out.

Things are looking complicated for couples – you might argue, and it might become something constant. This is not just any lovers' quarrel. One of you may tire of the constant tensions and start to wonder - "What am I really getting out of this?"

Health. In March, you are not particularly energetic, and should be especially careful if you are elderly or suffer from chronic disease. If this is you, the stars recommend being very attentive to your own body and not overdoing it.

Young and healthy Libras might feel tired of constant pressure at work, and the stars recommend that you find the time to relax and be sure to get enough sleep. These are easy ways to calm your nerves and any irritability.

March is the ideal time for any wellness activities, such as massage, some light cosmetic procedures, or simply spending time in nature.

April

New York Time				London Time		
Calendar Day	Lunar Day	Lunar Day Start Time		Calendar Day	Lunar Day	Lunar Day Start Time
01/04/2022	1	1:27 AM		01/04/2022	30	6:41 AM
01/04/2022	2	5:49 AM		01/04/2022	1	7:27 AM
02/04/2022	3	6:17 AM		02/04/2022	2	7:00 AM
03/04/2022	4	6:47 AM		03/04/2022	3	7:21 AM
04/04/2022	5	7:19 AM		04/04/2022	4	7:45 AM
05/04/2022	6	7:55 AM		05/04/2022	5	8:14 AM
06/04/2022	7	8:37 AM		06/04/2022	6	8:49 AM
07/04/2022	8	9:23 AM		07/04/2022	7	9:32 AM
08/04/2022	9	10:14 AM		08/04/2022	8	10:23 AM
09/04/2022	10	11:10 AM		09/04/2022	9	11:22 AM
10/04/2022	11	12:09 PM		10/04/2022	10	12:26 PM
11/04/2022	12	1:11 PM		11/04/2022	11	1:35 PM
12/04/2022	13	2:14 PM		12/04/2022	12	2:46 PM
13/04/2022	14	3:19 PM		13/04/2022	13	4:00 PM
14/04/2022	15	4:26 PM		14/04/2022	14	5:15 PM
15/04/2022	16	5:35 PM		15/04/2022	15	6:33 PM
16/04/2022	17	6:46 PM		16/04/2022	16	7:54 PM
17/04/2022	18	7:59 PM		17/04/2022	17	9:16 PM
18/04/2022	19	9:12 PM		18/04/2022	18	10:39 PM
19/04/2022	20	10:23 PM		19/04/2022	19	11:58 PM
20/04/2022	21	11:29 PM		21/04/2022	20	1:07 AM
22/04/2022	22	12:25 AM		22/04/2022	21	2:04 AM
23/04/2022	23	1:13 AM		23/04/2022	22	2:48 AM
24/04/2022	24	1:53 AM		24/04/2022	23	3:21 AM
25/04/2022	25	2:28 AM		25/04/2022	24	3:48 AM
26/04/2022	26	2:58 AM		26/04/2022	25	4:10 AM
27/04/2022	27	3:25 AM		27/04/2022	26	4:29 AM
28/04/2022	28	3:52 AM		28/04/2022	27	4:47 AM
29/04/2022	29	4:19 AM		29/04/2022	28	5:05 AM
30/04/2022	30	4:47 AM		30/04/2022	29	5:25 AM
30/04/2022	1	4:30 PM		30/04/2022	1	9:30 PM

You can find the description of each lunar day in the chapter "A Guide to The Moon Cycle and Lunar Days"

April is a great time for slow, analytical, painstaking tasks, as well as business or personal meetings. Make some real plans in order to take advantage of this.

Work. Entrepreneurs and managers will be busy getting everything in order for their teams. You will need to check the work of some longtime employees, as well as new arrivals – this will be the bulk of your workdays this month.

Entrepreneurs and managers will also have to find a way to get rid of those who are holding you back unnecessarily, and closely consider who is hardworking and professional. Naturally, you have been considering that for a while now, though the time has come to take another step forward in order to improve your team's work and breathe new life into it.

Employees have a great opportunity to improve their position, and if that recently happened, then April is a great time to strengthen that gain. This is the perfect month for meetings, new people, and discussing financial issues. The latter is important for anyone seeking to expand his or her business.

Money. April is a good time for your bank account. Money is coming in regularly, and you can expect to receive the largest sums on April 8, 9, 17, 18, and 25-27.

In addition to your normal income, you can expect some successful credit and loan negotiations, as well as help from a sponsor. Those who are not part of the business world can count on help from loved ones, a spouse, or parents.

Love and family. When it comes to family and your love life, try not to go against the flow, and carefully consider your loved ones' interests – in this case, your relationship is beginning a new phase of understanding, trust, and love.

Single people might meet someone interesting at work, on your team, or among new employees. In April, the stars are giving the green light to any office romances.

Couples who are getting along might see activities related to new real estate or rehabbing their current dwelling.

Health. In April, you are a bit sluggish, so take care of yourself and strive to live a healthy lifestyle. This is a good time to get a massage, visit a spa, or otherwise engage in some self-care.

You can consider your lifestyle and say no to any bad habits if you have any, and keep an eye out for any diseases. After all, you can't be too careful!

May

New York Time			London Time		
Calendar Day	Lunar Day	Lunar Day Start Time	Calendar Day	Lunar Day	Lunar Day Start Time
01/05/2022	2	6:18 AM	01/05/2022	2	5:48 AM
02/05/2022	3	6:53 AM	02/05/2022	3	6:14 AM
03/05/2022	4	7:32 AM	03/05/2022	4	6:47 AM
04/05/2022	5	8:16 AM	04/05/2022	5	7:27 AM
05/05/2022	6	9:06 AM	05/05/2022	6	8:14 AM
06/05/2022	7	10:00 AM	06/05/2022	7	9:10 AM
07/05/2022	8	10:57 AM	07/05/2022	8	10:12 AM
08/05/2022	9	11:57 AM	08/05/2022	9	11:18 AM
09/05/2022	10	12:59 PM	09/05/2022	10	12:27 PM
10/05/2022	11	2:02 PM	10/05/2022	11	1:38 PM
11/05/2022	12	3:06 PM	11/05/2022	12	2:51 PM
12/05/2022	13	4:13 PM	12/05/2022	13	4:07 PM
13/05/2022	14	5:22 PM	13/05/2022	14	5:25 PM
14/05/2022	15	6:34 PM	14/05/2022	15	6:47 PM
15/05/2022	16	7:49 PM	15/05/2022	16	8:11 PM
16/05/2022	17	9:03 PM	16/05/2022	17	9:34 PM
17/05/2022	18	10:14 PM	17/05/2022	18	10:50 PM
18/05/2022	19	11:16 PM	18/05/2022	19	11:55 PM
20/05/2022	20	12:10 AM	20/05/2022	20	12:46 AM
21/05/2022	21	12:53 AM	21/05/2022	21	1:24 AM
22/05/2022	22	1:30 AM	22/05/2022	22	1:53 AM
23/05/2022	23	2:01 AM	23/05/2022	23	2:16 AM
24/05/2022	24	2:30 AM	24/05/2022	24	2:36 AM
25/05/2022	25	2:56 AM	25/05/2022	25	2:54 AM
26/05/2022	26	3:23 AM	26/05/2022	26	3:12 AM
27/05/2022	27	3:50 AM	27/05/2022	27	3:31 AM
28/05/2022	28	4:20 AM	28/05/2022	28	3:52 AM
29/05/2022	29	4:53 AM	29/05/2022	29	4:17 AM
30/05/2022	30	5:30 AM	30/05/2022	30	4:47 AM
30/05/2022	1	7:32 AM	30/05/2022	1	12:32 PM
31/05/2022	2	6:13 AM	31/05/2022	2	5:24 AM

You can find the description of each lunar day in the chapter "A Guide to The Moon Cycle and Lunar Days"

This month is a good time to take a deep breath and focus on the little details or various administrative tasks, both at home and at work.

Work. May is not a very promising time when it comes to major projects at work. It is worth focusing on administrative tasks, where you are facing a lot of difficulties.

Entrepreneurs and managers will have to monitor their employees, who are decisive and hardworking, right now. The main issue is that these qualities do have their limits, and making sure they are not working against what you had originally planned.

Jupiter is changing position, which means that very soon, you will be surrounded by new people. If you meet them between May 10 and June 3, though, be very careful- they will likely not be particularly useful, and may even turn out to be a source of trouble. However, your relationship with previous partners and friends might reach a new level of trust and understanding.

During this time, Mercury will be in retrograde, and based on thousands of years of astrological observations, this is a bad time for new acquaintances or signing any important documents. It might be a good time for you to slow down and keep going with something you started earlier, or simply take some vacation time.

Employees should remember that discipline, responsibility, and teamwork will go a long way. It might also be a good time for you to take a few days to work on the house or spend time with your children and family.

Money. May is not a bad time for your wallet. You might be receiving money from work you have done, as well as various unofficial sources.

Those who are not part of the business world can count on support from loved ones who are doing very well for themselves at work

You can count on the largest sums of money on May 1, 5, 6, 15-16, 23, 24, 28, and 29.

Love and family. Things in your personal life are going swimmingly. You might even strike a healthy balance between work and family life, this month. You have worked hard and done a lot, and it is finally time to think about those close to you. You might strengthen that harmonious relationship by taking a trip together.

Jupiter's shifting this month will mean wonderful news for single people. Very soon, your circle of friends will expand, and you will find someone who will turn out to be a major support for you in the long term.

But remember – that is not the case from May 10 to June 2. Mercury will be in retrograde, and any new people you meet during this period might turn out to bring nothing but disappointment. Remember, not all that glitters is gold, and be mindful.

Health. In May, you will occasionally feel down and unsure of yourself. When that happens, try taking a trip to your summer home, spending time in nature, or, if you can, get a massage on a tropical beach.

June

New York Time			London Time		
Calendar Day	Lunar Day	Lunar Day Start Time	Calendar Day	Lunar Day	Lunar Day Start Time
01/06/2022	3	7:00 AM	01/06/2022	3	6:09 AM
02/06/2022	4	7:53 AM	02/06/2022	4	7:02 AM
03/06/2022	5	8:49 AM	03/06/2022	5	8:02 AM
04/06/2022	6	9:48 AM	04/06/2022	6	9:06 AM
05/06/2022	7	10:48 AM	05/06/2022	7	10:14 AM
06/06/2022	8	11:49 AM	06/06/2022	8	11:23 AM
07/06/2022	9	12:51 PM	07/06/2022	9	12:33 PM
08/06/2022	10	1:55 PM	08/06/2022	10	1:45 PM
09/06/2022	11	3:01 PM	09/06/2022	11	3:00 PM
10/06/2022	12	4:10 PM	10/06/2022	12	4:18 PM
11/06/2022	13	5:22 PM	11/06/2022	13	5:39 PM
12/06/2022	14	6:37 PM	12/06/2022	14	7:03 PM
13/06/2022	15	7:50 PM	13/06/2022	15	8:24 PM
14/06/2022	16	8:58 PM	14/06/2022	16	9:36 PM
15/06/2022	17	9:58 PM	15/06/2022	17	10:35 PM
16/06/2022	18	10:47 PM	16/06/2022	18	11:20 PM
17/06/2022	19	11:28 PM	17/06/2022	19	11:54 PM
19/06/2022	20	12:03 AM	19/06/2022	20	12:20 AM
20/06/2022	21	12:33 AM	20/06/2022	21	12:42 AM
21/06/2022	22	1:00 AM	21/06/2022	22	1:01 AM
22/06/2022	23	1:27 AM	22/06/2022	23	1:19 AM
23/06/2022	24	1:54 AM	23/06/2022	24	1:38 AM
24/06/2022	25	2:23 AM	24/06/2022	25	1:58 AM
25/06/2022	26	2:54 AM	25/06/2022	26	2:21 AM
26/06/2022	27	3:30 AM	26/06/2022	27	2:49 AM
27/06/2022	28	4:11 AM	27/06/2022	28	3:24 AM
28/06/2022	29	4:57 AM	28/06/2022	29	4:06 AM
28/06/2022	1	10:53 PM	29/06/2022	1	3:53 AM
29/06/2022	2	5:48 AM	29/06/2022	2	4:56 AM
30/06/2022	3	6:43 AM	30/06/2022	3	5:54 AM

You can find the description of each lunar day in the chapter "A Guide to The Moon Cycle and Lunar Days"

Jupiter is shifting in the sky, and once again that is leading to changes in your life. This has both pluses and minuses, and it's out of your hands – that's life!

Work. This month, you are seeing new opportunities open their doors. The astrologist predicts that many of them will be related to your business partners who will support you both morally and materially. You can rest assured that their role in your business will be a positive thing. Despite the obvious good will of your colleagues, as well as their responsibility, there might sometimes be feelings of dependence, which in these situations, is only natural, though it is not always the most pleasant thing.

If that is the case, remember, safety in numbers, and whenever possible, sit down and carefully discuss the terms of future cooperation.

Your ties with colleagues from other cities or abroad are moving along nicely, and you might take a successful trip in June.

Money. Your financial position is stable, though you are getting most of your income from business partners, and possibly some interest-free credit. Those who are not part of the business world can count on help from a loved one who is currently on a lucky streak at work.

Love and family. Many Libras will be focused on events at home, involving their family or romantic relationships.

Spouses who are getting along will take on important household tasks together and resolve them. Fortunately, the costs will be covered by a loved one who is on an unusually positive streak and ready to share their success with the whole family.

Single people and those who have been let down by relationships in the past will meet new people in their social circles, you might start an interesting romance, and it might end in marriage.

Those who are in a relationship might make things permanent.

Any trips you take in June are likely to be unusually successful and strengthen your relationship, whether you are married or not.

Health. In June, you are healthy, energetic, charming, and witty. Everyone Fate places on your path is noticing, too. You will forget about your health for a bit, which is usually a good sign that all is well.

July

New York Time			London Time		
Calendar Day	Lunar Day	Lunar Day Start Time	Calendar Day	Lunar Day	Lunar Day Start Time
01/07/2022	4	7:41 AM	01/07/2022	4	6:57 AM
02/07/2022	5	8:41 AM	02/07/2022	5	8:04 AM
03/07/2022	6	9:41 AM	03/07/2022	6	9:12 AM
04/07/2022	7	10:42 AM	04/07/2022	7	10:22 AM
05/07/2022	8	11:44 AM	05/07/2022	8	11:32 AM
06/07/2022	9	12:47 PM	06/07/2022	9	12:44 PM
07/07/2022	10	1:53 PM	07/07/2022	10	1:58 PM
08/07/2022	11	3:01 PM	08/07/2022	11	3:15 PM
09/07/2022	12	4:13 PM	09/07/2022	12	4:35 PM
10/07/2022	13	5:25 PM	10/07/2022	13	5:56 PM
11/07/2022	14	6:35 PM	11/07/2022	14	7:12 PM
12/07/2022	15	7:40 PM	12/07/2022	15	8:18 PM
13/07/2022	16	8:35 PM	13/07/2022	16	9:10 PM
14/07/2022	17	9:21 PM	14/07/2022	17	9:50 PM
15/07/2022	18	9:59 PM	15/07/2022	18	10:20 PM
16/07/2022	19	10:32 PM	16/07/2022	19	10:45 PM
17/07/2022	20	11:02 PM	17/07/2022	20	11:05 PM
18/07/2022	21	11:29 PM	18/07/2022	21	11:25 PM
19/07/2022	22	11:57 PM	19/07/2022	22	11:43 PM
21/07/2022	23	12:25 AM	21/07/2022	23	12:03 AM
22/07/2022	24	12:56 AM	22/07/2022	24	12:26 AM
23/07/2022	25	1:31 AM	23/07/2022	25	12:52 AM
24/07/2022	26	2:10 AM	24/07/2022	26	1:25 AM
25/07/2022	27	2:54 AM	25/07/2022	27	2:04 AM
26/07/2022	28	3:43 AM	26/07/2022	28	2:52 AM
27/07/2022	29	4:37 AM	27/07/2022	29	3:47 AM
28/07/2022	30	5:35 AM	28/07/2022	30	4:49 AM
28/07/2022	1	1:55 PM	28/07/2022	1	6:55 PM
29/07/2022	2	6:34 AM	29/07/2022	2	5:55 AM
30/07/2022	3	7:35 AM	30/07/2022	3	7:04 AM
31/07/2022	4	8:36 AM	31/07/2022	4	8:13 AM

You can find the description of each lunar day in the chapter "A Guide to The Moon Cycle and Lunar Days"

This month, you can count on real progress toward reaching your goals. In the heavens, the roads are clear, with no traffics or accidents on the horizon.

Work. You are looking at an active, hardworking, and eventful month. Business partners with power and influence might play an important role in work-related events. That is, a team is coming together, and that will play a big role in your ability to significantly improve your position both this year and next.

However, working with others will involve making some concessions, and you will have to do the same. You may have disagreements on your shared business, but they should be resolved by August.

Your relationship with colleagues from other cities or abroad is developing nicely, and you might go on a successful trip where you hold constructive negotiations. It is worth carefully watching this area, as a bit later, in the fall, you might experience misunderstandings and have to revisit your current discussions. This may occur several times, and you need to be prepared for what might be coming.

Likewise, managers and entrepreneurs should keep a close eye on their subordinates, who may not be giving you what you need. In some cases, that may be due to laziness and incompetence, but in others, it may be a case of deception and sabotage. That is the weak link in your work, and it may cause endless problems later on.

Employees will periodically deal with intrigue from their colleagues and competition, but can count on managers supporting them. It is worth bringing up any issues like this.

Money. Your bank account is looking healthy in July. In addition to your usual income, you can count on support from business partners, dividends from the bank, and beneficial terms of credit. Those who are not part of the business world will receive help from parents, loved ones, and spouses.

Love and family. Your personal life is also looking rather eventful. A loved one is experiencing a lot of success at work, and he or she may support you in either words or deeds. You may experience some minor quarrels this month, maybe due to differing views on household matters or your children's education. You may have disagreements on construction, repairs, or rehabilitating an old home.

Your relationship with children is still demanding a lot of attention. Saturn, the planet of responsibility and discipline, is demanding you keep a closer eye on your children and support them if they need it.

Jupiter, which is firmly in the sector of the sky related to relationships, is lucky for single people. If you still haven't found anyone suitable, he or she is sure to appear- in some cases, it will last a long time, and in others, forever.

Any vacations you take will be successful, but it is better to plan them for the end of the months or in August. That is when you will have time for yourself and it is worth taking full advantage of it! As they say, you deserve it!

Health. In July, you are health, active, and up for adventure. You may even forget all about your health, which is always a good sign all is well.

August

New York Time			London Time		
Calendar Day	Lunar Day	Lunar Day Start Time	Calendar Day	Lunar Day	Lunar Day Start Time
01/08/2022	5	9:37 AM	01/08/2022	5	9:23 AM
02/08/2022	6	10:40 AM	02/08/2022	6	10:34 AM
03/08/2022	7	11:44 AM	03/08/2022	7	11:46 AM
04/08/2022	8	12:49 PM	04/08/2022	8	1:00 PM
05/08/2022	9	1:58 PM	05/08/2022	9	2:17 PM
06/08/2022	10	3:07 PM	06/08/2022	10	3:35 PM
07/08/2022	11	4:16 PM	07/08/2022	11	4:51 PM
08/08/2022	12	5:22 PM	08/08/2022	12	6:00 PM
09/08/2022	13	6:20 PM	09/08/2022	13	6:58 PM
10/08/2022	14	7:10 PM	10/08/2022	14	7:43 PM
11/08/2022	15	7:52 PM	11/08/2022	15	8:17 PM
12/08/2022	16	8:28 PM	12/08/2022	16	8:45 PM
13/08/2022	17	9:00 PM	13/08/2022	17	9:07 PM
14/08/2022	18	9:29 PM	14/08/2022	18	9:28 PM
15/08/2022	19	9:57 PM	15/08/2022	19	9:47 PM
16/08/2022	20	10:26 PM	16/08/2022	20	10:07 PM
17/08/2022	21	10:56 PM	17/08/2022	21	10:29 PM
18/08/2022	22	11:30 PM	18/08/2022	22	10:54 PM
20/08/2022	23	12:08 AM	19/08/2022	23	11:25 PM
21/08/2022	24	12:50 AM	21/08/2022	24	12:02 AM
22/08/2022	25	1:38 AM	22/08/2022	25	12:46 AM
23/08/2022	26	2:30 AM	23/08/2022	26	1:39 AM
24/08/2022	27	3:27 AM	24/08/2022	27	2:39 AM
25/08/2022	28	4:26 AM	25/08/2022	28	3:45 AM
26/08/2022	29	5:27 AM	26/08/2022	29	4:53 AM
27/08/2022	1	4:16 AM	27/08/2022	30	6:02 AM
27/08/2022	2	6:28 AM	27/08/2022	1	9:16 AM
28/08/2022	3	7:30 AM	28/08/2022	2	7:13 AM
29/08/2022	4	8:33 AM	29/08/2022	3	8:24 AM
30/08/2022	5	9:37 AM	30/08/2022	4	9:36 AM
31/08/2022	6	10:42 AM	31/08/2022	5	10:50 AM

You can find the description of each lunar day in the chapter "A Guide to The Moon Cycle and Lunar Days"

This month, the impossible becomes possible – you are able to do it all. And that goes for work, leisure, and your personal life.

Work. In August, many Libras find themselves at the epicenter of a whirlwind of activity, both pleasant and less-so.

The first half of the month is a good time to work on your contacts and meet new people, too. In order to seek new partners, you need support, and there's no better time to find it. Things change quickly, however, and by the second half of August, there are dark clouds looming on the horizon.

Your relationship with like-minded people, friends, or the powers that be is about to become much more complicated. You may experience some significant confrontation when it comes to ethical or financial issues. This situation will continue into the fall, so there is good reason to deal with the problems now, and not put them off until later. Do what you can and dig in for the long fight.

The last week of August will have you busy with a variety of organizational tasks, and this will continue into September.

Money. For many Libras, August is a ruinous month. You will be bleeding money in all directions – vacation, travel, kids, household and professional tasks – it will all require a huge amount of resources, more than you initially intended.

On the other hand, friends and powers that be will be insisting you pay them back what you owe, and this will also not come cheap. As a result, by the end of the month, many Libras will find themselves with empty pockets.

Love and family. August is a great time for vacations, outdoor parties, shopping, and traveling around the world. If you want to spend money, this is the time to do it. The best time for all of this is the first half of the month.

The second half of August will be more challenging, and you might face a litany of problems related to your children, which, naturally, require money to resolve.

For couples, the second half of August is also a test of endurance. You may face unexpected disagreements, possibly about differing viewpoints on various issues, or perhaps about money. For example, if you start to become stingy, you will not be able to avoid problems. So decide which is more important- love or money.

The last few days of the month, many Libras will be dealing with dull household matters, and this will continue into September.

Health. All month long, you are feeling energetic, charming, and attractive. Naturally, with those qualities, there's no time for falling ill!

September

New York Time			London Time		
Calendar Day	Lunar Day	Lunar Day Start Time	Calendar Day	Lunar Day	Lunar Day Start Time
01/09/2022	7	11:49 AM	01/09/2022	6	12:06 PM
02/09/2022	8	12:57 PM	02/09/2022	7	1:23 PM
03/09/2022	9	2:05 PM	03/09/2022	8	2:38 PM
04/09/2022	10	3:10 PM	04/09/2022	9	3:48 PM
05/09/2022	11	4:10 PM	05/09/2022	10	4:48 PM
06/09/2022	12	5:01 PM	06/09/2022	11	5:37 PM
07/09/2022	13	5:45 PM	07/09/2022	12	6:14 PM
08/09/2022	14	6:23 PM	08/09/2022	13	6:44 PM
09/09/2022	15	6:56 PM	09/09/2022	14	7:08 PM
10/09/2022	16	7:26 PM	10/09/2022	15	7:30 PM
11/09/2022	17	7:55 PM	11/09/2022	16	7:50 PM
12/09/2022	18	8:24 PM	12/09/2022	17	8:10 PM
13/09/2022	19	8:54 PM	13/09/2022	18	8:31 PM
14/09/2022	20	9:27 PM	14/09/2022	19	8:55 PM
15/09/2022	21	10:04 PM	15/09/2022	20	9:24 PM
16/09/2022	22	10:45 PM	16/09/2022	21	9:58 PM
17/09/2022	23	11:31 PM	17/09/2022	22	10:40 PM
19/09/2022	24	12:22 AM	18/09/2022	23	11:30 PM
20/09/2022	25	1:17 AM	20/09/2022	24	12:28 AM
21/09/2022	26	2:15 AM	21/09/2022	25	1:31 AM
22/09/2022	27	3:15 AM	22/09/2022	26	2:38 AM
23/09/2022	28	4:17 AM	23/09/2022	27	3:47 AM
24/09/2022	29	5:19 AM	24/09/2022	28	4:58 AM
25/09/2022	30	6:22 AM	25/09/2022	29	6:10 AM
25/09/2022	1	5:54 PM	25/09/2022	1	10:54 PM
26/09/2022	2	7:27 AM	26/09/2022	2	7:23 AM
27/09/2022	3	8:33 AM	27/09/2022	3	8:38 AM
28/09/2022	4	9:40 AM	28/09/2022	4	9:54 AM
29/09/2022	5	10:49 AM	29/09/2022	5	11:12 AM
30/09/2022	6	11:58 AM	30/09/2022	6	12:29 PM

You can find the description of each lunar day in the chapter "A Guide to The Moon Cycle and Lunar Days"

September is one of the most difficult months of your year. Hold on and remember that you've got to break a few eggs to make an omelet!

Work. In September, many Libras may find themselves on the receiving end of a lot of spite and ill will. In some cases, that may mean disagreements with a business partner who promised one thing and then did quite another – or maybe nothing at all. Or maybe colleagues in other cities or abroad are behaving irresponsibly or maliciously. This conflict will become part of the background in your life in September and for the next several months.

Entrepreneurs and managers should keep a close eye on subordinates – one of them may still be playing their own game, which will lead to serious damages for your reputation and business. This may not be the first time, either, so watch your employees like a hawk.

What's more, a lot of things may have happened in secret without you noticing, and you will only learn about them in mid-September. Keep your finger on the pulse of things and look around for any weak points. This is relevant for entrepreneurs and employees alike, as competitors of all stripes may be sabotaging your work. Keep your eyes open and avoid gossip.

Money. Financially speaking, this month is not particularly promising, but that is no surprise given everything going on at work. Expect a lot of expenses and less income than usual, so avoid spending if you can and watch both your money and those around you.

Love and family. If your personal life is more important to you, get ready for some trouble here, too. Problems can appear out of thin air and still knock you off your feet.

Spouses with old grudges will be surprised to discover their partner is ready to take decisive action and unwilling to give in at all. Your attempts at smoothing things over will be seen as weakness and lead nowhere. If relatives get involved in your argument, things will get even worse.

Unmarried couples will also experience an unexpected deterioration in their relationship – especially if you find yourselves torn between two options. In September, some secrets will come to light, and you will not be able to sidestep a scandal! Remember that and take precautions. Remember that whatever happens in September will have longstanding and decisive consequences, so if you are planning any big changes at work or in your personal life, think things over again.

Health. Those who have managed to escape trouble at home or at work might find it in their health. In September, there is a high likelihood of old, chronic diseases flaring up again, and you might face some unexpected and new problems, as well. Be very careful when traveling or driving. The last 20 days of the month are the most dangerous.

October

New York Time			London Time		
Calendar Day	Lunar Day	Lunar Day Start Time	Calendar Day	Lunar Day	Lunar Day Start Time
01/10/2022	7	1:04 PM	01/10/2022	7	1:41 PM
02/10/2022	8	2:04 PM	02/10/2022	8	2:44 PM
03/10/2022	9	2:57 PM	03/10/2022	9	3:35 PM
04/10/2022	10	3:43 PM	04/10/2022	10	4:15 PM
05/10/2022	11	4:21 PM	05/10/2022	11	4:46 PM
06/10/2022	12	4:55 PM	06/10/2022	12	5:11 PM
07/10/2022	13	5:25 PM	07/10/2022	13	5:33 PM
08/10/2022	14	5:54 PM	08/10/2022	14	5:53 PM
09/10/2022	15	6:23 PM	09/10/2022	15	6:12 PM
10/10/2022	16	6:52 PM	10/10/2022	16	6:33 PM
11/10/2022	17	7:24 PM	11/10/2022	17	6:55 PM
12/10/2022	18	7:59 PM	12/10/2022	18	7:22 PM
13/10/2022	19	8:39 PM	13/10/2022	19	7:54 PM
14/10/2022	20	9:23 PM	14/10/2022	20	8:34 PM
15/10/2022	21	10:12 PM	15/10/2022	21	9:21 PM
16/10/2022	22	11:06 PM	16/10/2022	22	10:16 PM
18/10/2022	23	12:03 AM	17/10/2022	23	11:17 PM
19/10/2022	24	1:02 AM	19/10/2022	24	12:22 AM
20/10/2022	25	2:03 AM	20/10/2022	25	1:30 AM
21/10/2022	26	3:04 AM	21/10/2022	26	2:39 AM
22/10/2022	27	4:06 AM	22/10/2022	27	3:50 AM
23/10/2022	28	5:10 AM	23/10/2022	28	5:03 AM
24/10/2022	29	6:16 AM	24/10/2022	29	6:18 AM
25/10/2022	1	6:48 AM	24/10/2022	30	7:35 AM
25/10/2022	2	7:25 AM	25/10/2022	1	11:48 AM
26/10/2022	3	8:35 AM	25/10/2022	2	8:54 AM
27/10/2022	4	9:46 AM	26/10/2022	3	10:14 AM
28/10/2022	5	10:55 AM	27/10/2022	4	11:30 AM
29/10/2022	6	11:59 AM	28/10/2022	5	12:38 PM
30/10/2022	7	12:55 PM	29/10/2022	6	12:33 PM
31/10/2022	8	1:42 PM	30/10/2022	7	1:16 PM
			31/10/2022		

You can find the description of each lunar day in the chapter "A Guide to The Moon Cycle and Lunar Days"

You can't move further until you've made peace with the past. The stars urge you to learn the lessons from your own mistakes, especially if you made them more than once. October is the best time to do it!

Work. Many Libras went through a dark period in September, and the clouds are beginning to clear. Difficult relationships with colleagues in other cities or abroad are slowly, but surely becoming predictable again. Of course, there are still some issues there, and it is worth paying attention to them, given that this has long been an area of turbulence in your professional life. There's no point in letting up just yet.

The stars recommend that you back up any agreements with colleagues in other cities or abroad with something tangible, like a signed contract. If things change, you can always back yourself up with this and remind your unreliable partners. If they'll go for it, of course.

Any trips planned for October will be very successful.

Managers and entrepreneurs should keep a close eye on their subordinates. They seem unreliable, incompetent, and possibly even dishonest at the worst possible time.

Employees should be careful with colleagues so long as things keep brewing on your team. In order to avoid any potential intrigue and gossip, you need to clearly identify who is a friend, who is an enemy, who is not a friend but not an enemy, etc.... and generally behave with more caution.

If you have any problems with someone from work, take it right to your management – there will be some opportunities to rectify things there.

Overall, October will be much better for you than September, and largely thanks to your own hard work.

Money. Your financial position is also looking up, especially as you get closer to the end of October. The largest sum will come in on October 25-28.

You have a lot of expenses, and the astrologist predicts this will be related to your personal and family life. You are improving your home, your children might have some more financial needs again, but the stars believe that closer to the end of the month, you will be back in the black.

Love and family. Your personal life is looking shaky and uneven right now. Parents are probably dealing with problems involving their children, who once again (!) are incurring huge expenses. You might have to pony up for your adult children's training and education, but if you don't do it, who will?

In the worst cases, you will have to resolve your children's problems, which will also require resources, effort, and nerves on your part.

Couples who get along will possibly spend a lot of money near the end of the month on home improvements. You may also be completing tasks like finishing a new home, buying furniture, or acquiring other items for your home décor.

Your relationship with your partner is far from ideal – you might have some major fights, and any reconciliation will be fragile. In order to build harmony in your relationships, you might take a trip together – you will definitely have an opportunity to do so.

Health. In October, you are feeling a lot more energetic than you were, and any illnesses from last month are sure to quickly pass.

November

New York Time			London Time		
Calendar Day	Lunar Day	Lunar Day Start Time	Calendar Day	Lunar Day	Lunar Day Start Time
01/11/2022	9	2:23 PM	01/11/2022	8	1:50 PM
02/11/2022	10	2:57 PM	02/11/2022	9	2:16 PM
03/11/2022	11	3:27 PM	03/11/2022	10	2:38 PM
04/11/2022	12	3:56 PM	04/11/2022	11	2:58 PM
05/11/2022	13	4:24 PM	05/11/2022	12	3:17 PM
06/11/2022	14	3:52 PM	06/11/2022	13	3:36 PM
07/11/2022	15	4:22 PM	07/11/2022	14	3:58 PM
08/11/2022	16	4:56 PM	08/11/2022	15	4:22 PM
09/11/2022	17	5:33 PM	09/11/2022	16	4:52 PM
10/11/2022	18	6:16 PM	10/11/2022	17	5:28 PM
11/11/2022	19	7:04 PM	11/11/2022	18	6:12 PM
12/11/2022	20	7:56 PM	12/11/2022	19	7:05 PM
13/11/2022	21	8:52 PM	13/11/2022	20	8:03 PM
14/11/2022	22	9:50 PM	14/11/2022	21	9:07 PM
15/11/2022	23	10:49 PM	15/11/2022	22	10:13 PM
16/11/2022	24	11:49 PM	16/11/2022	23	11:21 PM
18/11/2022	25	12:50 AM	18/11/2022	24	12:30 AM
19/11/2022	26	1:52 AM	19/11/2022	25	1:41 AM
20/11/2022	27	2:56 AM	20/11/2022	26	2:53 AM
21/11/2022	28	4:03 AM	21/11/2022	27	4:09 AM
22/11/2022	29	5:13 AM	22/11/2022	28	5:27 AM
23/11/2022	30	6:25 AM	23/11/2022	29	6:48 AM
23/11/2022	1	5:57 PM	23/11/2022	1	10:57 PM
24/11/2022	2	7:37 AM	24/11/2022	2	8:08 AM
25/11/2022	3	8:45 AM	25/11/2022	3	9:23 AM
26/11/2022	4	9:47 AM	26/11/2022	4	10:25 AM
27/11/2022	5	10:39 AM	27/11/2022	5	11:15 AM
28/11/2022	6	11:23 AM	28/11/2022	6	11:52 AM
29/11/2022	7	12:00 PM	29/11/2022	7	12:21 PM
30/11/2022	8	12:31 PM	30/11/2022	8	12:45 PM

You can find the description of each lunar day in the chapter "A Guide to The Moon Cycle and Lunar Days"

In November, if you can't do everything, you can do the vast majority of what you dream up. A new chapter is about to begin in your life.

Work. This month, you will be incredibly busy at work. Right now, you in a state of not eating, drinking, or sleeping, and doing nothing but putting your nose to the grindstone.

In some areas, managers and entrepreneurs can boldly count on their subordinates, and in others, they will have to resolve things singlehandedly. The former includes current tasks and administrative matters. But it is worth keeping a firm grip on your relationship with colleagues from other cities or abroad, who may send things into yet another tailspin.

This is an area where you often run into difficulties, and you may already know exactly what you need to do. Right now, it is worth keeping an eye on resistance from your opponents, which will probably not end quickly, this time – you can expect a few months of negotiations and active confrontation and intrigue.

Entrepreneurs and managers should prepare for an audit, as it is highly likely by the end of this month.

Money. Money-wise, November is not bad. Many Libras will be flush with money, cash, and other material benefits.

Expect the largest sums on November 3, 4, 11-13, 22, and 23. However, as often happens, with income you also have expenses. Many will have to pay back debts, deal with family needs, and support a spouse or partner. As before, a significant chunk of your family budget is going toward your children's needs.

Love and family. Your personal life is looking both emotional and turbulent in November. You might not have time to be dealing with matters of the heart at all, and a loved one will bring various complaints and demands to you.

Alternatively, you may see a lot of resistance when it comes to money

– what and how to spend your family budget. There is nothing wrong with you having differing ideas, but an argument is inevitable.

Things are more difficult for those who are dating – in the best-case scenario, they might not see each other as often as they would like, but in the worst-case, they may unexpectedly realize that they are very different in certain areas. If your relationship is important to you, then you will have to learn to compromise. If not, it's time for the train to leave the station.

Many Libras will deal with various problems involving relatives. Most likely, this involves your in-laws. Nothing here is new, but this time, things are more difficult and taking longer to resolve. That may be due to arguments, or possible challenges related to close family members.

Health. In November, you are feeling a bit sluggish, but you will avoid any major complications if you follow a schedule and do morning exercises.

Elderly people and those who are weakened by disease should take preventive measures against any chronic conditions and take care of themselves, avoiding any autumn colds and infections.

December

New York Time			London Time		
Calendar Day	Lunar Day	Lunar Day Start Time	Calendar Day	Lunar Day	Lunar Day Start Time
01/12/2022	9	1:00 PM	01/12/2022	9	1:05 PM
02/12/2022	10	1:27 PM	02/12/2022	10	1:24 PM
03/12/2022	11	1:55 PM	03/12/2022	11	1:42 PM
04/12/2022	12	2:24 PM	04/12/2022	12	2:03 PM
05/12/2022	13	2:56 PM	05/12/2022	13	2:25 PM
06/12/2022	14	3:31 PM	06/12/2022	14	2:53 PM
07/12/2022	15	4:11 PM	07/12/2022	15	3:26 PM
08/12/2022	16	4:57 PM	08/12/2022	16	4:07 PM
09/12/2022	17	5:48 PM	09/12/2022	17	4:56 PM
10/12/2022	18	6:42 PM	10/12/2022	18	5:53 PM
11/12/2022	19	7:40 PM	11/12/2022	19	6:55 PM
12/12/2022	20	8:39 PM	12/12/2022	20	8:00 PM
13/12/2022	21	9:38 PM	13/12/2022	21	9:07 PM
14/12/2022	22	10:37 PM	14/12/2022	22	10:15 PM
15/12/2022	23	11:37 PM	15/12/2022	23	11:23 PM
17/12/2022	24	12:39 AM	17/12/2022	24	12:32 AM
18/12/2022	25	1:42 AM	18/12/2022	25	1:44 AM
19/12/2022	26	2:49 AM	19/12/2022	26	2:59 AM
20/12/2022	27	3:58 AM	20/12/2022	27	4:18 AM
21/12/2022	28	5:10 AM	21/12/2022	28	5:38 AM
22/12/2022	29	6:22 AM	22/12/2022	29	6:56 AM
23/12/2022	1	5:17 AM	23/12/2022	30	8:07 AM
23/12/2022	2	7:28 AM	23/12/2022	1	10:17 AM
24/12/2022	3	8:27 AM	24/12/2022	2	9:04 AM
25/12/2022	4	9:17 AM	25/12/2022	3	9:49 AM
26/12/2022	5	9:58 AM	26/12/2022	4	10:22 AM
27/12/2022	6	10:32 AM	27/12/2022	5	10:49 AM
28/12/2022	7	11:03 AM	28/12/2022	6	11:11 AM
29/12/2022	8	11:31 AM	29/12/2022	7	11:30 AM
30/12/2022	9	11:59 AM	30/12/2022	8	11:49 AM
31/12/2022	10	12:28 PM	31/12/2022	9	12:09 PM

You can find the description of each lunar day in the chapter "A Guide to The Moon Cycle and Lunar Days"

You tend to play by the rules and expect the same out of others. However, it is wise to remember that if you want peace, you need to prepare for war.

Work. Your relationship with partners from other cities or abroad will be your greatest task this month. Here, everything will once again be difficult, and this time, you may be pushed to your limits. You are unlikely to find a peaceful resolution to things, as there is too much conflict lately on both sides. During the first half of December, you might even think about totally cutting ties.

Your relationship with subordinates will also be a problem this month. This is a difficult issue that has come up in the past, but nonetheless you are unable to count on certain team members.

Don't discount the possibility that your decisions will not be carried out, or carried out in such a way that does not live up to your expectations. If that is your case, managers at every level should stick to their guns and watch everything happening on their team like a hawk.

In December, you might be inspected or audited, so be ready to defend yourself on all fronts. You are a tough cookie, you'll get through it!

Money. December is a rather neutral time for your finances. Your troubles at work will not be reflected in your bank account, at least for now. Expect to receive the largest sums on December 1, 2, 9-11, 20, 21, 27, and 28.

Love and family. In your personal life, you can expect problems with those around you. In many cases, you will see the emergence or continuation of problems with close relatives. In some cases, there may be an argument, and nearly every family member will be dragged into it. Alternatively, a relative might fall ill or go through a difficult time and that will be reflected in the entire family ambiance.

This month, many Virgos will see things brought to light you would have preferred to keep quiet. That may affect your relationship with loved ones and cause serious fights, too. In all relationships, the first half of December is the hardest time, before the skies begin to clear.

Health. In December, you are cheerful, energetic, and incredibly active. The stars still recommend that you take care when driving and traveling.

During the first half of the month, the stars urge you to avoid traveling, whether near or far from home, as this will bring you nothing but trouble. Wait until a more favorable time, such as the second half of December.

A Guide to The Moon Cycle and Lunar Days

Since Ancient times, people have noticed that the moon has a strong influence on nature. Our Earth and everything living on it is a single living being, which is why the phases of the moon have such an effect on our health and mental state, and therefore, our lives. Remember Shakespeare and his description of Othello's jealousy in his famous tragedy:

"It is the very error of the moon, She comes more nearer Earth than she was wont And makes men mad."

If our inner rhythm is in harmony with that of the cosmos, we are able to achieve much more. People were aware of this a thousand years ago. The lunar calendar is ancient. We can find it among the ancient Sumerians (4000-3000 BC), the inhabitants of Mesopotamia, Native Americans, Hindus, and ancient Slavs. There is evidence that the Siberian Yakuts had a lunar calendar, as did the Malaysians.

Primitive tribes saw the moon as a source of fertility. Long before Christianity, the waxing moon was seen as favorable for planting new crops and starting a new business, for success and making money, while the waning moon was a sign that business would end.

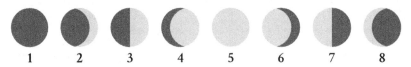

What are the phases of the moon?

- Phase 1 – new moon
- Phase 2 – waxing crescent moon
- Phase 3 – first quarter moon
- Phase 4 – waxing gibbous moon
- Phase 5 – full moon
- Phase 6 – waning gibbous moon
- Phase 7 – third quarter moon
- Phase 8 – waning crescent moon

To simplify things, we can divide the month into two phases:
Waxing crescent moon - before the full moon
Waning crescent moon - after the full moon

New Moon

We cannot see the new moon, as it is hidden. People might complain about feeling weak, mental imbalance, and fatigue. During this time, we want to avoid taking on too much or overdoing things. Generally, people are not very responsive and react poorly to requests, which is why it is best to look out for yourself, while not keeping your plate too full.

The new moon is a bad time for advertising – it will go unnoticed. It is not worth preparing any presentations, parties, or loud gatherings. People are feeling constrained, not very social, and sluggish.

This is also a less than ideal time for surgery, as your recovery will be slow, and the likelihood of medical error is high.

It is also difficult to get an accurate diagnosis during the new moon – diseases might seem to be hidden, and doctors might not see the real underlying cause of what ails you.

The new moon is also a bad time for dates, and sexual encounters may be dissatisfying and leave you feeling disappointed. Ancient astrologers did not advise planning a wedding night during the new moon.

Waxing Crescent Moon

It is easy to identify a waxing crescent moon. If you draw an imaginary line between the two "horns", you should see the letter P. The waxing moon is then divided into one and two quarters.

During the first quarter moon, we need to focus on planning – setting goals and thinking of how we will set about achieving them. However, it is still a good idea to hold back a bit and not overdo things. Energy levels are still low, though they are growing along with the moon. It is still a good idea to avoid any medical procedures during this time.

The second quarter is a time for bold, decisive action. Things will come easy, and there is a greater chance of a lucky break. This is a good time for weddings, especially if the moon will be in Libra, Cancer, or Taurus. Nevertheless, it is a good idea to put off any advertising activities and public speaking until closer to the full moon, if you can.

Full Moon

During the full moon, the Earth is located between the sun and the moon. During this time, the moon is round and fully illuminated. This takes place during days 14-16 of the lunar cycle.

During the full moon, many people feel more vigorous than usual. They are emotional, sociable, and actively seeking more contact, so this may be a good time for any celebrations.

However, be careful not to drink too much – you can relax to the point that you lose control, and the consequences of that can be very unpleasant. If you are able to stick to moderation, there is no better time for a party!

The full moon is also the best time for advertising, as not only will your campaign be widely seen, people will be apt to remember it.

The full moon is also a favorable time for dates, and during this time, people are at their most open, romantic, and willing to tell each other something important that might take their relationship to the next level of trust and understanding.

Moreover, during the full moon, people feel a surge of energy, which may lead to hyperactivity, restlessness, and insomnia.

It will be harder to keep your emotions in check. You might face conflicts with friends, disasters, and accidents. During the full moon, any surgeries are **not a good idea**, as the risk of complications and bleeding is on the rise. Plastic surgery is also a bad idea, as swelling and bruises might be much worse than in another lunar phase. At the same time, the full moon is a good time to get an accurate diagnosis.

During this time, try to limit your calories and liquid intake (especially if you deal with bloating and excess weight), as your body is absorbing both calories and liquids faster during the full moon, and it can be very difficult to get rid of the weight later on.

Waning Crescent Moon

The full moon is over, and a new phase is beginning – the waning moon. This is a quieter time, when all of the jobs you started earlier are being partly or entirely completed (it all depends on the speed and scale).

Surgery will turn out much better if it is performed during the waning moon. Your recovery will be faster, and the likelihood of complications is much lower. If you have any plans to lose weight, the waning moon is the best time to do that. This is also a good time for quitting bad habits, such as smoking or cursing.

The waning moon can also be divided into the third and fourth quarters.

Third quarter - this is a favorable period, and you are able to resolve a lot of problems without conflict. People are calming down and ready to listen and take in information, while still being active. However, this is not the best time to begin any major projects, especially if you are unsure if you will be able to complete them by the start of the new lunar month.

The third quarter is a good time to get married, especially if the moon is in Cancer, Taurus, or Libra.

Fourth quarter – This is the most passive period of the lunar cycle. You are not as strong as usual. Your energy is lagging. You will be tired until reaching a new beginning. The best thing you can do as the lunar cycle comes to an end is to get things in order, and avoid anything that might get in your way at work or in personal relationships. Examine your successes and failures.

Now, let's discuss the lunar days in greater detail. For centuries, people around the world have described the influence of lunar days, and modern astrologers only add to this work, as they compare old texts to modern life.

The 1ˢᵗ lunar day

The first lunar day is extremely important for the rest of the lunar month. This is a much-needed day to carefully plan your activities and lay the groundwork for the rest of the lunar month. Remember that the first lunar day is not a good day for major activities, but rather for sitting down and planning things.

Avoid conflicts on this day, unless you want them to overshadow the rest of the month. Try to see the positive side of things and imagine that the lunar month will bring you good things both at work and in love. The more vividly you can imagine this, the sooner your desires will come to fruition. Perhaps it would be a good idea to jot down plans that will bring you closer to achieving your dreams. This is the best time for both manifesting and making wishes!

This is also a favorable day when it comes to seeking a new job or starting an academic program.

It is fine to go out on a date on the first lunar day, but limit any sexual contact, as your energy levels are low, and you are likely to end up disappointed.

Getting married on the first lunar day is not recommended.

Avoid getting a haircut – there are many indications that cutting your hair on the first lunar day will have a negative effect on your health and life expectancy.

Under no circumstances should you undergo any major cosmetic procedures, including plastic surgery. Energy levels are low, your skin is dull and almost stagnant. The results will not live up to your expectations, and in the worst-case scenario, you will end up looking worse than before. It is common for cosmetic procedures performed on this day to be disappointing or even useless. Even the best surgeons are less capable.

Your good dreams on the first lunar day foretell happiness and joy. Bad ones usually do not come true.

The 2ⁿᵈ lunar day

This is considered a lucky day, and is symbolized by a cornucopia. It is not an exaggeration to say that the second lunar day is a favorable time for both work and love. It is a time for action, and a great period to work on yourself, look for a new job, start something new, or complete any financial transaction, whether a sale or purchase. This is also a great time for creative and scientific insights, and a good time for any meeting – whether political or romantic.

Any romantic dates or sexual encounters during the second lunar day are unlikely to disappoint. This is also a good day for weddings or taking a trip with someone special.

During the second lunar day, the moon is beginning its waxing phase, which is a good time for anything you might to do nourish and restore your skin. This is a great time for any cosmetic procedures aimed at preservation, though it is best to put off any plastic surgery until the waning moon. If that is not possible, then the second lunar day is acceptable, if not ideal, and you will not run into any complications.

Folklore tells us that this is not a good day for a haircut, as that may lead to arguments with a loved one.

This is the best time for exercise – your body is in good shape, and you are able to handle new exercise regimens. If the moon happens to be in Scorpio, though, be careful.

This is a good day for anything positive, but avoid any conflicts, discussions about the status of your relationship, or litigation.

Dreams of the second lunar day are usually not prophetic.

The 3rd lunar day

On this day, we are usually able to make out a thin sliver of the lunar crescent. It is a longstanding tradition to show money during the new month – it is believed that as the moon grows, so will your savings.

However, astrological systems around the world consider this an unlucky, unfavorable day. It is not a good idea to travel, begin any new business, or give into your bad mood.

You might run into many a lot of problems at work on this day, which will cause you a lot of anxiety. However, it is a good day to take a step back and identify and set about fixing any flaws and shortcomings. Remember that everything tends to look worse on this day than it actually is.

It is not the time to ask management for anything – you are likely to walk away disappointed, and end up unfairly reprimanded rather than receiving a promotion or raise. Instead, focus on areas of work that need to be smoothed over or studied further. It will be clear what problems you are facing, and you will easily be able to find a remedy.

Do not rush to criticize your loved ones – things may not be as they appear. "Measure twice and cut once" is your motto on this day.

This is not a good day to get married, as the couple is likely to have a turbulent, short-lived marriage.

You can schedule a cosmetic procedure for this day, but only if it is relatively minor. Plastic surgery should wait.

Do exercises as usual, without overdoing it or adding any new routines.

Dreams on this day do not mean anything.

The 4th lunar day

These are relatively neutral days, in that they are unlikely to bring anything bad, but they also will not bring you any windfalls. The fourth lunar day is symbolized by a tree of paradise, the tree of knowledge, and the choice between good and evil. Things ultimately depend on us and our final decisions.

This is a great day for anything money-related – signing contracts, agreements, or even taking on credit. There are also a lot of contradictions on this day – on one hand, we are likely to receive money, which is a good thing, but on the other, we will have to give some of it away, which is never particularly fun or pleasant. There is good reason to consider all of your opportunities and possibilities before acting.

It is not a good day to get married, as the wedding will not be as fun as you had hoped. However, the fourth lunar day is, in fact, a good day for sex and conceiving a healthy child.

Be careful on this day if you happen to engage in any physical exercise, as it is not a good idea to overeat or abuse alcohol. Take care of yourself. Any illnesses which began on this day may be extremely dangerous, if they are not dealt with immediately.

Cosmetic procedures are not contraindicated, as long as they are to preserve your appearance. Plastic surgery can be performed if you truly feel it is necessary.

However, avoid getting a haircut, as it is unlikely to grow back healthily, and will become brittle and dull. However, if the moon is in Leo, you can disregard this advice.

Dreams may turn out to be real.

The 5th lunar day

Traditionally, the fifth lunar day is one of the worst of the lunar month. It is symbolized by a unicorn. Unicorns need to be tamed, but only a virgin is capable of doing so. Many people will feel drained on this day, or frustrated with themselves, those around them, and life in general.

Try to avoid arguments- any conflicts are likely to drag out for a long time, and then you may be overcome with guilt. This advice is relevant for both work and love.

Sexual encounters may be pleasant, but this is not a good day to plan a wedding, as it is likely to lead to a marriage full of unpleasant incidents.

Do not start any new businesses, or ask those around you for favors- you may be misunderstood and rejected.

It is fine to engage in physical exercise, but if you overdo it on this day, you may injure yourself.

Your energy levels are low. Cosmetic procedures may not be effective, and avoid any plastic surgeries.

It is good if you dream something connected with the road, trips or with movement in general. A bad dream might be a sign of a health problem which should be addressed.

The 6th lunar day

The symbol of the sixth lunar day is a cloud and a crane. This is a philosophical combination that suggests that it is not worth rushing things on these days. This is a very positive, lucky day for both work and love. Creative work will be especially successful, as will any attempts at opening a new business in your field.

The sixth lunar day is a good time for resolving any financial matters. There is one limitation, however – do not give anyone a loan, as they may not pay it back. But you can certainly sponsor and support those who are more vulnerable than you.

This day is a good time to go on a trip, whether close to home or far away.

This is also a good day for dates, weddings, and marriage proposals. Remember that energy is more romantic than sexual, so it is better to give the gift of roses and a bottle of champagne than hot, passionate sex.

It is a good idea to get some exercise, but do not overdo things, though you will probably not want to, either.

Cosmetic procedures will be successful, and you can even have plastic surgery performed, so long as the moon is not in Scorpio.

It is still a good idea to avoid getting your hair cut, as you might "cut off" something good in addition to your hair.

It is better to not discuss dreams as they are usually true. Your dreams of this day can remind you of something that needs to be completed as soon as possible.

The 7th lunar day

This is also a favorable lunar day, and it is symbolized by a fighting cock, which is an Avestan deity. Avoid any aggression on this day, and instead work on yourself, spend time at home or in nature. Avoid discussing the status of your relationship with anyone, arguing, or wishing bad things on anyone. Everything will come back to haunt you, remember, silence is golden.

Business negotiations and contracts will be successful. You can find support, sponsors, and people ready to help you in both words and deeds.

Lighten up with your colleagues and subordinates. Pay attention not only to their shortcomings, but also to their skills. This is a good day for reconciliation and creating both political and romantic unions.

The seventh lunar day is good for traveling, no matter how near or far from home.

It is also a favorable time for love and marriage.

Exercise moderately, and any plastic surgeries will go very smoothly, as long as the moon is not in Scorpio.

Dreams of this day may become a reality.

The 8th lunar day

The symbol for this day is a Phoenix, which symbolizes eternal rebirth and renewal, because this day is a great time for changes in all areas of your life. Your energy is likely to be high, and you want to do something new and unusual. This is a good time to look for a new job or begin studying something. Any out-of-the-box thinking is welcome, along with shaking things up a bit in order to improve your life.

However, avoid any financial transactions, as you may incur losses.

Avoid aggression. You can share your opinion by presenting well-founded arguments and facts, instead.

The phoenix rises from the ashes, so this is a good time to be careful with electrical appliances and fire in general. The risk of housefires is high.

Avoid any major financial transactions on the eighth day, as you may end up facing a series of complications. You can pay people their salaries, as this is unlikely to be a large sum.

This is a good day for weddings, but only if you and your future spouse are restless, creative souls and hope to achieve personal development through your marriage.

Any cosmetic procedures and plastic surgeries will go well today, as they are related to rebirth and renewal. Surgeons may find that they are true artists on this day!

You can try to change your hairstyle and get a fashionable haircut on this day.

You can trust your dreams seen on this day.

The 9th lunar day

The ninth lunar day is not particularly auspicious, and is even referred to as "Satan's" day. You may be overcome with doubt, suspicions, even depression and conflicts.

Your self-esteem will suffer, so don't overdo things physically, and avoid overeating or abusing alcohol.

This is a negative day for any business deals, travel, or financial transactions.

This is a particularly bad day for any events, so keep your head down at work and avoid any new initiatives.

It is better to avoid getting married on "Satan's" day, as the marriage will not last very long. Avoid sex, as well, but you can take care of your partner, listen them, and support them however they need.

Any cosmetic procedures will not have a lasting effect, and avoid any plastic surgery. A haircut will not turn out as you hoped.

Dreams of this day are usually prophetic.

The 10th lunar day

This is one of the luckiest days of the lunar month. It is symbolized by a spring, mushroom, or phallus. This is a time for starting a new business, learning new things, and creating.

The 10th lunar day is particularly lucky for business. Networking and financial transactions will be a success and bring hope. This is an ideal time for changing jobs, shifting your business tactics, and other renewals.

This is a perfect time for people in creative fields and those working in science, who may come up with incredible ideas that will bring many successful returns.

This is a very successful day for building a family and proposing marriage. This is a good time for celebrations and communication, so plan parties, meet with friends, and plan a romantic date.

One of the symbols for this day is a phallus, so sexual encounters are likely to be particularly satisfying.

The 10th lunar day is the best time to begin repairs, buying furniture, and items for home improvement.

You can exercise vigorously, and cosmetic procedures and plastic surgery will be very effective.

Dreams of this day will not come true.

The 11th lunar day

This is one of the best lunar days, and seen as the pinnacle of the lunar cycle. People are likely to be energetic, enthusiastic, and ready to move forward toward their goals.

The 11th lunar day is very successful for any financial transactions or business deals and meetings.

You might actively make yourself known, approach management to discuss a promotion, or look for a new job. This is an auspicious time for advertising campaigns, performances, and holding meetings.

Any trips planned will be a great success, whether near or far from home.

Romantic relationships are improving, sex is harmonious, and very desired.

Weddings held on this day will be fun, and the marriage will be a source of joy and happiness.

Exercise is a great idea, and you might even beat your own personal record.

This is an ideal time for any cosmetic procedures, but any more serious plastic surgeries might lead to a lot of bruising and swelling.

A haircut will turn out as you had hoped, and you can experiment a bit with your appearance.

You can ignore dreams of this day – usually they do not mean anything.

The 12th lunar day

This day is symbolized by the Grail and a heart. As we move closer to the full moon, our emotions are at their most open. During this time, if you ask someone for something, your request will be heeded. This is a day of faith, goodness, and divine revelations.

For business and financial transactions, this is not the most promising day. However, if you help others on this day, your good deeds are sure to come back to you.

This is a day for reconciliation, so do not try to explain your relationships, as no one is at fault, and it is better to focus on yourself, anyway.

Avoid weddings and sex on this day, but if you want to do what your partner asks, there is no better time.

Many may feel less than confident and cheerful during this day, so take it easy when working out. Avoid overeating, stay hydrated, and avoid alcohol.

The 12th lunar day is not the best for getting married or having sex, but the stars would welcome affection and a kind word.

Avoid getting a haircut, or any plastic surgeries. This is a neutral day for minor cosmetic procedures.

Nearly all dreams will come true.

The 13th lunar day

This day is symbolized by Samsara, the wheel of fate, which is very erratic and capable of moving in any direction. This is why the 13th lunar day is full of contradictions. In Indian traditions, this day is compared to a snake eating its own tail. This is a day for paying off old debts and returning to unfinished business.

Avoid beginning any new business on this day. It is preferable to finish old tasks and proofread your work. Information you receive on this day may not be reliable and must be verified.

It is worth resolving financial problems very carefully, and avoid arguments and conflict.

Do not change jobs on this day or go to a new place for the first time. Do not sit at home alone, though, go see old friends, parents, or older family members.

Minor cosmetic procedures are welcome on this day, but avoid any plastic surgery, as you may experience major swelling and bruising. Avoid any haircuts, too.

As a rule, all dreams will come true.

The 14th lunar day

It's a full moon! The 14th lunar day is one of the happiest, and it is symbolized by the trumpet. Pay attention – you may run into new, much-needed information. Networking will be successful, and you can confidently sign agreements, meet with people, and attend fun gatherings or other leisure activities. This is one of the best days for advertising, performances, and concerts, and those working in creative professions should keep this in mind, as should those who work in politics. Do not sit in place on this day – you need to get out and see others, make new connections, and try to be visible.

This is one of the best days for communication with and making requests from management, as your initiatives will be noticed and welcome. You might talk about a promotion, raise, or something similarly related to professional growth.

Couples will see their relationship is moving along well on this day, and it is also a good day for getting married.

Any sex on this day will be vigorous and memorable for a long time. The full moon is the best time for conceiving a child.

Any cosmetic procedures will be effective, but avoid any major changes to your appearance, as there is a high likelihood of bleeding and bruising. A haircut will turn out well.

Your dreams of this day will be more or less doubtful.

The 15th lunar day

It's a full moon! This day is symbolized by a serpent of fire. This is the energy peak of the entire lunar cycle, and a lot will depend on where you are focusing your energy.

You might face a lot of temptations on this day, for example, you might tell someone else's secret or your own to others, and come to regret it for a long time. The stars suggest exercising restraint in both your words and actions, as the 15th day of the lunar cycle is a day of deception and weaknesses.

This is a very active time, and many people might take unnecessary risks. This is not the best day for signing any agreements or contracts. For any performances, concerts, or advertising, however, this is one of the best days of the month.

You can get married on the 15th day, but only if you know each other well and have carefully considered your partnership, without any hasty decisions. This is also a favorable day for a second marriage.

Your romantic relationship is looking wonderful – you are on cloud 9, writing poetry, and deeply convinced of how right your partner is for you – and they feel the same way. It is important that this does not suddenly lead to an abrupt disappointment.

Avoid getting any haircuts on the 15th day of the month, as you may end up with a headache.

Conservative cosmetic procedures and creams will be very effective, but avoid any injections or plastic surgery today. Bleeding, swelling, and bruising are all but guaranteed.

Dreams on the 15th day nearly always come true.

The 16th lunar day

This day is symbolized by a dove. The full moon is over, and the moon is now in its waning phase. Usually, after the turbulent days of the full moon, people feel a bit under the weather. They are not cheerful, and want to avoid excess worry and give themselves a chance to breathe.

Don't ignore your body's wishes, take it easy with physical activities, and take some time for yourself. You might spend time in nature, in the forest, or at a country home.

The 16th day of the lunar month is a time for moderation in all areas – your behavior, eating, and even in your clothes. If you overate during the full moon period, now is the time to diet a bit or at least avoid fatty foods and meat.

This is not a promising day for resolving any financial matters. Keep your documents in order and get ready for any future meetings, instead. If you help a loved one, your good deed will come back 100 times over.

Avoid getting married today, as well as sex.

Cosmetic procedures are likely to be a success, especially if they are related to cleansing your skin, but it is best to avoid any plastic surgery or injections. Your body is not ready to accept them. A haircut will turn out as you hoped.

Any dreams are likely to come true, but that also depends on a correct interpretation.

The 17th lunar day

This day is represented by a vine and bell. It is a happy day and both successful and fun-filled. It is also a good time for negotiations, concluding small business deals, shaking up staffing, and creativity. However, you should keep in mind that the 17th day is only favorable for minor business, and you should avoid starting any major events.

Avoid any major financial transactions on this day. Do not give anyone money as a loan or borrow anything yourself, either.

Any travel, whether for business or pleasure, is likely to be a success.

The 17th day is a great time to get married, and an ideal day for dates. Any sexual encounters will bring you happiness and joy.

Avoid getting your hair cut on this day, but cosmetic procedures and plastic surgery will be a success. Women will look better than usual.

Your dreams are likely to come true in three days.

The 18th lunar day

This day is represented by a mirror. It is a difficult, and generally unpromising day, too. Just as the mirror reflects our imperfections back to us, we need to remember that moderation and modesty are key.

The 18th day is not a favorable time for any business meetings or financial transactions. You can, however work on jobs you already began. It is, however, a positive day for those who work in research or the creative fields.

Your motto of the day is to keep a cool head when it comes to your opportunities and the opportunities of those around you. This is relevant for both work and romantic relationships. It is not a good time to criticize others – any conflicts or arguments may lead to lasting consequences, which you do not need.

Avoid getting married on this day, as well as sexual encounters, which are likely to be disappointing. It is a good time to take a trip together, which will only be good for your relationship.

Avoid getting your hair cut, though this is a relatively neutral day for a haircut, which might turn out well, and though it will not exceed your expectations, it will also not leave you upset. Avoid any plastic surgeries.

Dreams on this day will come true.

The 19th lunar day

This is a very difficult day and it is represented by a spider. The energy is complicated, if not outright dangerous. Don't panic or get depressed, though – this is a test of your strength, and if you are able to hold onto all you have achieved. This is relevant for both work and love. On the 19th day, you should avoid taking any trips.

The energy of the 19th lunar day is very unfavorable for beginning any major projects, and business in general. Work on what you started earlier, get your affairs in order, think over your ideas and emotions, and check to make sure that everything you have done hitherto is living up to your expectations. Do not carry out any financial transactions or take out any loans – do not loan anyone else money, either. Do not ask your managers for anything as they are unlikely to listen to what you have to say, and make judgments instead.

This is a day when you might face outright deception, so do not take any risks and ignore rumors. Do not work on anything related to real estate or legal matters.

This is a very hard time for people with an unbalanced psyche, as they may experience sudden exacerbations or even suicidal ideations.

This is a very unlucky day to get married. Sexual encounters might be disappointing and significantly worsen your relationship.

Avoid any haircuts or cosmetic procedures or surgeries.

Your dreams of this day will come true.

The 20th lunar day

This is also a difficult day, though less so than the 19th. It is represented by an eagle. This is a good time to work on your own development and spiritual growth, by speaking to a psychologist or astrologer.

Avoid pride, anger, arrogance, and envy.

The 20th lunar day is a good time for people who are active and decisive. They will be able to easily overcome any obstacles, flying over them just like an eagle. If you have to overcome your own fears, you will be able to do so – don't limit yourself, and you will see that there is nothing to be afraid of. It is a good day for any financial transactions, signing contracts, and reaching agreements, as well as networking.

The 20th lunar day is a favorable time for those who work in the creative fields, as they will be able to dream up the idea that will open up a whole host of new possibilities. Avoid conflicts – they may ruin your relationship with a lot of people, and it will not be easy to come back from that.

This is a lucky day for getting married, but only if you have been with your partner for several years, now. Sexual encounters will not be particularly joyful, but they also will not cause you any problems.

Avoid getting your hair cut, but you can certainly get it styled. The 20th lunar day is a good day for those who are looking to lose weight. You will be able to do so quickly, and it will be easy for you to follow a diet.

Cosmetic procedures will be a success, as will any plastic surgeries.

Pay attention to dreams of this day as they are likely to come true.

The 21st lunar day

This is one of the most successful days of the lunar month, and it is symbolized by a herd of horses – imagine energy, strength, speed, and bravery. Everything you think up will happen quickly, and you will be able to easily overcome obstacles. A mare is not only brave but also an honest animal, so you will only experience this luck if you remember that honesty is always the best policy.

This is also a favorable day for business. Reaching new agreements and signing contracts, or dealing with foreign partners – it is all likely to be a success. Any financial issues will be resolved successfully.

Those in the creative world will be able to show off their talent and be recognized for their work. Anyone involved in the performing arts can expect success, luck, and recognition. A galloping herd of horses moves quickly, so you might transition to a new job, move to a new apartment, or go on a business trip or travel with your better half.

The 21st lunar day is one of the best to get married or have a sexual encounter.

This is a great time for athletes, hunters, and anyone who likes adventurous activities.

But for criminals and thieves, this is not a lucky or happy day – they will quickly be brought to justice.

Any haircuts or cosmetic procedures are likely to be a huge success and bring both beauty and happiness. You will recover quickly after any surgeries, perhaps without any swelling or bruising at all.

Dreams tend to not be reliable.

The 22nd lunar day

This day will be strange and contradictory. It is symbolized by the elephant Ganesha. According to Indian mythology, Ganesha is the patron saint of hidden knowledge. so this is a favorable day for anyone who is trying to learn more about the world and ready to find the truth, though this is often seen as a hopeless endeavor. This is a day for philosophers and wisemen and women. However, it is an inauspicious day for business, and unlikely to lead to resolving financial issues, signing contracts, agreements, or beginning new projects. You can expect trouble at work.

For creative people, and new employees, this is a successful day.

This is a good day for apologies and reconciliation.

Avoid getting married, though you can feel free to engage in sexual encounters.

For haircuts and cosmetic procedures, this is a fantastic day. Surgeries will also turn out, as long as the moon is not in Scorpio.

Dreams will come true.

The 23rd lunar day

This is a challenging day represented by a crocodile, which is a very aggressive animal. This is a day of strong energy, but it is also adventurous and tough. Your main task is to focus your energy in the right direction. There may be accidents, arguments, conflicts, fights, and violence, which is why it is important to strive for balance and calm.

Keep a close eye on your surroundings – there may be traitors or people who do not wish you well, so be careful.

However, this is still a favorable day for business – many problems will be resolved successfully. You are able to sign contracts and receive credit successfully, as long as you remain active and decisive in what you do.

This is not a day for changing jobs or working on real estate transactions or legal proceedings. This is not a favorable day for traveling, no matter how near or far you plan on going.

This is not a promising day to get married – things may end in conflict, if not an all-out brawl.

Sexual relations are not off the table, as long as the couple trusts one another.

Haircuts or cosmetic procedures will not turn out as you had hoped, so avoid them.

Dreams during this lunar day usually mean something opposite of what awaits you, so you can disregard them.

The 24th lunar day

This is a neutral, calm day that is symbolized by a bear. It is favorable for forgiveness and reconciliation.

This is also a good day for learning new things, reading, self-development, and taking time to relax in nature.

This is a great day for any type of financial activity, conferences, academic meetings, and faraway travel.

The 24th lunar day is a good time for love and getting married, as any marriage will be strong and lasting.

Cosmetic procedures and plastic surgery will be a success, and you can expect a speedy recovery.

Avoid getting a haircut on this day, however, as your hair will likely thin and grow back slowly.

Dreams of this lunar day are usually connected with your personal life.

The 25th lunar day

This is still another quiet day, symbolized by a turtle.

Just like a turtle, this is not a day to rush, and it is best to sit down and take stock of your life. This is a good time for resolving any personal problems, as the moon's energy makes it possible for you to calm down and find the right path.

This is also not a bad day for business. It is believed that any business you begin on this day is sure to be a success. This is especially the case for trade and any monetary activities.

The 25th lunar day is not a good day to get married, especially if the couple is very young.

This is a neutral day for sexual encounters, as the moon is waning, energy is low, so the decision is yours.

Avoid any cosmetic procedures, except those for cleansing your skin. This is not a favorable day for haircuts or plastic surgery – unless the moon is in Libra or Leo.

You can have a prophetic dream on this day.

The 26th lunar day

The 26th lunar day is full of contradictions and complicated. It is represented by a toad.

It is not time to start or take on something new, as nothing good will come of it. Avoid any major purchases, as you will later come to see that your money was wasted. The best thing you can do on this day is stay at home and watch a good movie or read a good book.

Avoid traveling on this day, as it may not turn out well.

The 26th lunar day is a negative day for any business negotiations and starting new businesses. Do not complete any business deals or financial transactions. Your colleagues may be arguing, and your managers may be dissatisfied. But if you have decided to leave your job, there is no better time to do so.

This is not a good day to get married, as both partners' expectations may fall flat, and they will soon be disappointed.

The waning moon carries a negative charge, so avoid any haircuts and surgeries, though you can get cosmetic procedures if they are relatively minor.

Your dreams will come true.

The 27th lunar day

The 27th lunar day is one of the best days of the month, and it is represented by a ship. You can boldly start any new business, which is sure to be promising. This is a great day for students, teachers, and learning new things. Any information that comes to you on this day may be extremely valuable and useful to you.

The 27th day is good for communication and travel, whether near or far from home, and no matter whether it is for work or pleasure.

This is also a good day for any professional activities or financial transactions. If there are people around you who need help, you must support them, as your good deeds will come back 100-fold.

Romantic dates will go well, though any weddings should be quiet and subdued. This is a particularly good day for older couples or second marriages.

The waning moon means that hair will grow back very slowly, but in general, you can expect a haircut to turn out well. This is a great day for plastic surgery or cosmetic procedures, as the results will be pleasing, and you will have a speedy recovery, without any bruising or swelling, most of the time.

However, beware if the moon is in Scorpio on this day – that is not a good omen for any plastic surgery.

Do not pay any attention to dreams on this day.

The 28ᵗʰ lunar day

This is another favorable day in the waning moon cycle, and it is represented by a lotus. This is a day of wisdom and spiritual awakening. If possible, spend part of the day in nature. It is important to take stock of the last month and decide what you need to do during its two remaining days.

This is a good time for any career development, changing jobs, conducting business, decision-making, and signing agreements, as well as going on a trip. You might conclude any business deal, hold negotiations, work with money and securities.

This is also a good day for any repairs or improvements around your home or apartment.

Any weddings today should be subdued and modest, and restricted to family members only. A loud, raucous wedding might not turn out very well.

Your hair will grow slowly, but any haircuts will turn out very elegant and stylish. Cosmetic procedures and surgeries are not contraindicated. You will recover quickly with little bruising and swelling.

Do not take any dreams too seriously.

The 29th lunar day

This is one of the most difficult days of the lunar month, and it is considered a Satanic day, unlucky for everyone and everything. It is symbolized by an octopus.

This is a dark day, and many will feel melancholy, depression, and a desire to simply be left alone. This is a day full of conflict and injuries, so be careful everywhere and with everyone. If you can, avoid any travel, and be particularly careful when handling any sharp objects. Do not engage in any business negotiations, sign any contracts, or take part in any networking.

Astrologers believe that anything you start on this day will completely fall apart. For once and for all, get rid of things that are impeding you from living your life. This is a good time to avoid people who you do find unpleasant.

This is also a time for fasting and limitations for everyone. Do not hold any celebrations, weddings, or have sexual relations – these events may not turn out as you hoped, and instead bring you nothing but suffering and strife.

Avoid getting a haircut, as well, as it will not make you look more beautiful and your hair will come back lifeless and dull. Cosmetic procedures can go ahead, but avoid any surgeries.

Dreams are likely to be true.

The 30th lunar day

There is not always a 30th lunar day, as some lunar months have only 29 days. This day is represented by a swan. The 30th lunar day is usually very short, and sometimes, it lasts less than an hour. This is a time for forgiveness and calm.

You might take stock of the last month, while also avoiding anything you do not need around you. Pay back loans, make donations, reconcile with those who recently offended you, and stop speaking to people who cause you suffering.

This is a good time for tying up loose ends, and many astrologers believe that it is also a good day to start new business.

However, avoid celebrations or weddings on this day. Spouses will either not live long, or they will quickly grow apart.

Do not get a haircut on this day, though cosmetic procedures are possible, as long as you avoid any surgeries.

Dreams promise happiness and should come true.

A Guide to Zodiac Compatibility

Often, when we meet a person, we get a feeling that they are good and we take an instant liking to them. Another person, however, gives us immediate feelings of distrust, fear and hostility. Is there an astrological reason why people say that 'the first impression is the most accurate'? How can we detect those who will bring us nothing but trouble and unhappiness?

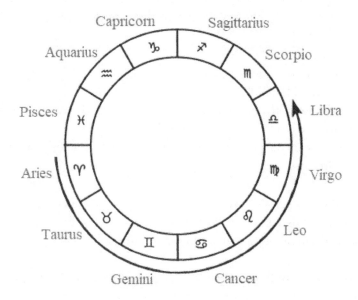

Without going too deeply into astrological subtleties unfamiliar to some readers, it is possible to determine the traits according to which friendship, love or business relationships will develop.

Let's begin with problematic relationships - our most difficult are with our **8th sign**. For example, for Aries the 8th sign is Scorpio, for Taurus it is Sagittarius and so on. Finding your 8th sign is easy; assume your own sign to be first (see above Figure) and then move eight signs counter clockwise around the Zodiac circle. This is also how the other signs (fourth, ninth and so on) that we mention are to be found.

Ancient astrologers variously referred to the 8th sign as the symbol of death, of destruction, of fated love or unfathomable attraction. In astrological terms, this pair is called 'master and slave' or 'boa constrictor and rabbit', with the role of 'master' or 'boa constrictor' being played by our 8th sign.

This relationship is especially difficult for politicians and business people.

We can take the example of a recent political confrontation in the USA. Hilary Clinton is a Scorpio while Donald Trump is a Gemini - her 8th sign. Even though many were certain that Clinton would be elected President, she lost.

To take another example, Hitler was a Taurus and his opponents – Stalin and Churchill - were both of his 8th sign, Sagittarius. The result of their confrontation is well known. Interestingly, the Russian Marshals who dealt crushing military blows to Hitler and so helped end the Third Reich - Konstantin Rokossovsky and Georgy Zhukov - were also Sagittarian, Hitler's 8th sign.

In another historical illustration, Lenin was also a Taurus. Stalin was of Lenin's 8th sign and was ultimately responsible for the downfall and possibly death of his one-time comrade-in-arms.

Business ties with those of our 8th sign are hazardous as they ultimately lead to stress and loss; both financial and moral. So, do not tangle with your 8th sign and never fight with it - your chances of winning are remote!

Such relationships are very interesting in terms of love and romance, however. We are magnetically attracted to our 8th sign and even though it may be very intense physically, it is very difficult for family life; 'Feeling bad when together, feeling worse when apart'.

As an example, let us take the famous lovers - George Sand who was Cancer and Alfred de Musset who was Sagittarius. Cancer is the 8th sign for Sagittarius, and the story of their crazy two-year love affair was the subject of much attention throughout France. Critics and writers were divided into 'Mussulist' and 'Sandist' camps; they debated fiercely about who was to blame for the sad ending to their love story - him or her. It's hard to imagine the energy needed to captivate the public for so long, but that energy was destructive for the couple. Passion raged in their hearts, but neither of them was able to comprehend their situation.

Georges Sand wrote to Musset, "*I ◆on't love you anymore, an◆ I will always a◆ore you. I ◆on't want you anymore, an◆ I can't ◆o without you. It seems that nothing but a heavenly lightning strike can heal me by ◆estroying me. Goo◆-bye! Stay or go, but ◆on't say that I am not suffering. This is the only thing that can make me suffer even more, my love, my life, my bloo◆! Go away, but kill me, leaving.*" Musset replied only in brief, but its power surpassed Sand's tirade, "*When you embrace◆ me, I felt something that is still bothering me, making it impossible for me to approach another woman.*" These two people loved each other passionately and for two years lived together in a powder keg of passion, hatred and treachery.

When someone enters into a romantic liaison with their 8th sign, there will be no peace; indeed, these relationships are very attractive to those who enjoy the edgy, the borderline and, in the Dostoevsky style, the melodramatic. The first to lose interest in the relationship is, as a rule, the 8th sign.

If, by turn of fate, our child is born under our 8th sign, they will be very different from us and, in some ways, not live up to our expectations. It may be best to let them choose their own path.

In business and political relationships, the combination with our **12th sign** is also a complicated one.

We can take two political examples. Angela Merkel is a Cancer while Donald Trump is a Gemini - her 12th sign. This is why their relations are strained and complicated and we can even perhaps assume that the American president will achieve his political goals at her expense. Boris

Yeltsin (Aquarius) was the 12th sign to Mikhail Gorbachev (Pisces) and it was Yeltsin who managed to dethrone the champion of Perestroika.

Even ancient astrologers noticed that our relationships with our 12th signs can never develop evenly; it is one of the most curious and problematic combinations. They are our hidden enemies and they seem to be digging a hole for us; they ingratiate themselves with us, discover our innermost secrets. As a result, we become bewildered and make mistakes when we deal with them. Among the Roman emperors murdered by members of their entourage, there was an interesting pattern - all the murderers were the 12th sign of the murdered.

We can also see this pernicious effect in Russian history: the German princess Alexandra (Gemini) married the last Russian Tsar Nicholas II (Taurus) - he was her 12th sign and brought her a tragic death. The wicked genius Grigory Rasputin (Cancer) made friends with Tsarina Alexandra, who was his 12th sign, and was murdered as a result of their odd friendship. The weakness of Nicholas II was exposed, and his authority reduced after the death of the economic and social reformer Pyotr Stolypin, who was his 12th sign. Thus, we see a chain of people whose downfall was brought about by their 12th sign.

So, it makes sense to be cautious of your 12th sign, especially if you have business ties. Usually, these people know much more about us than we want them to and they will often reveal our secrets for personal gain if it suits them. However, the outset of these relationships is, as a rule, quite normal - sometimes the two people will be friends, but sooner or later one will betray the other one or divulge a secret; inadvertently or not.

In terms of romantic relationships, our 12th sign is gentle, they take care of us and are tender towards us. They know our weaknesses well but accept them with understanding. It is they who guide us, although sometimes almost imperceptibly. Sexual attraction is usually strong.

For example, Meghan Markle is a Leo, the 12th sign for Prince Harry, who is a Virgo. Despite Queen Elizabeth II being lukewarm about the match, Harry's love was so strong that they did marry.

If a child is our 12th sign, it later becomes clear that they know all our secrets, even those that they are not supposed to know. It is very difficult to control them as they do everything in their own way.

Relations with our 7th **sign** are also interesting. They are like our opposite; they have something to learn from us while we, in turn, have something to learn from them. This combination, in business and personal relationships, can be very positive and stimulating provided that both partners are quite intelligent and have high moral standards but if not, constant misunderstandings and challenges follow. Marriage or co-operation with the 7th sign can only exist as the union of two fully-fledged individuals and in this case love, significant business achievements and social success are possible.

However, the combination can be not only interesting, but also quite complicated.

An example is Angelina Jolie, a Gemini, and Brad Pitt, a Sagittarius. This is a typical bond with a 7th sign - it's lively and interesting, but rather stressful. Although such a couple may quarrel and even part from time to time, never do they lose interest in each other.

This may be why this combination is more stable in middle-age when there is an understanding of the true nature of marriage and partnership. In global, political terms, this suggests a state of eternal tension - a cold war - for example between Yeltsin (Aquarius) and Bill Clinton (Leo).

Relations with our 9th **sign** are very good; they are our teacher and advisor - one who reveals things we are unaware of and our relationships with them very often involve travel or re-location. The combination can lead to spiritual growth and can be beneficial in terms of business.

Although, for example, Trump and Putin are political opponents, they can come to an understanding and even feel a certain sympathy for each other because Putin is a Libra while Trump is a Gemini, his 9th sign.

This union is also quite harmonious for conjugal and romantic relationships.

We treat our **3rd sign** somewhat condescendingly. They are like our younger siblings; we teach them and expect them to listen attentively. Our younger brothers and sisters are more often than not born under this sign. In terms of personal and sexual relationships, the union is not very inspiring and can end quickly, although this is not always the case. In terms of business, it is fairly average as it often connects partners from different cities or countries.

We treat our **5th sign** as a child and we must take care of them accordingly. The combination is not very good for business, however, since our 5th sign triumphs over us in terms of connections and finances, and thereby gives us very little in return save for love or sympathy. However, they are very good for family and romantic relationships, especially if the 5th sign is female. If a child is born as a 5th sign to their parents, their relationship will be a mutually smooth, loving and understanding one that lasts a lifetime.

Our **10th sign** is a born leader. Depending on the spiritual level of those involved, both pleasant and tense relations are possible; the relationship is often mutually beneficial in the good times but mutually disruptive in the bad times. In family relations, our 10th sign always tries to lead and will do so according to their intelligence and upbringing.

Our **4th sign** protects our home and can act as a sponsor to strengthen our financial or moral positions. Their advice should be heeded in all cases as it can be very effective, albeit very unobtrusive. If a woman takes this role, the relationship can be long and romantic, since all the spouse's wishes are usually met one way or another. Sometimes, such couples achieve great social success; for instance, Hilary Clinton, a Scorpio is the 4th sign to Bill Clinton, a Leo. On the other hand, if the husband is the 4th sign for his wife, he tends to be henpecked. There is often a strong sexual attraction. Our 4th sign can improve our living conditions and care for us in a parental way. If a child is our 4th sign, they are close to us and support us affectionately.

Relations with our **11th sign** are often either friendly or patronizing; we treat them reverently, while they treat us with friendly condescension. Sometimes, these relationships develop in an 'older brother' or 'high-ranking friend' sense; indeed, older brothers and sisters are often our 11th sign. In terms of personal and sexual relationships, our 11th sign is always inclined to enslave us. This tendency is most clearly manifested in such alliances as Capricorn and Pisces or Leo and Libra. A child who is the 11th sign to their parents will achieve greater success than their parents, but this will only make the parents proud.

Our **2nd sign** should bring us financial or other benefits; we receive a lot from them in both our business and our family life. In married couples, the 2nd sign usually looks after the financial situation for the benefit of the family. Sexual attraction is strong.

Our **6th sign** is our 'slave'; we always benefit from working with them and it's very difficult for them to escape our influence. In the event of hostility, especially if they have provoked the conflict, they receive a powerful retaliatory strike. In personal relations, we can almost destroy them by making them dance to our tune. For example, if a husband doesn't allow his wife to work or there are other adverse family circumstances, she gradually becomes lost as an individual despite being surrounded by care. This is the best-case scenario; worse outcomes are possible. Our 6th sign has a strong sexual attraction to us because we are the fatal 8th sign for them; we cool down quickly, however, and often make all kinds of demands. If the relationship with our 6th sign is a long one, there is a danger that routine, boredom and stagnation will ultimately destroy the relationship. A child born under our 6th sign needs particularly careful handling as they can feel fear or embarrassment when communicating with us. Their health often needs increased attention and we should also remember that they are very different from us emotionally.

Finally, we turn to relations with **our own sign**. Scorpio with Scorpio and Cancer with Cancer get along well, but in most other cases, however, our own sign is of little interest to us as it has a similar energy. Sometimes, this relationship can develop as a rivalry, either in business or in love.

There is another interesting detail - we are often attracted to one particular sign. For example, a man's wife and mistress often have the same sign. If there is confrontation between the two, the stronger character displaces the weaker one. As an example, Prince Charles is a Scorpio, while both Princess Diana and Camilla Parker Bowles were born under the sign of Cancer. Camilla was the more assertive and became dominant.

Of course, in order to draw any definitive conclusions, we need an individually prepared horoscope, but the above always, one way or another, manifests itself.

Love Description of Zodiac Signs

We know that human sexual behavior has been studied at length. Entire libraries have been written about it, with the aim of helping us understand ourselves and our partners. But is that even possible? It may not be; no matter how smart we are, when it comes to love and sex, there is always an infinite amount to learn. But we have to strive for perfection, and astrology, with its millennia of research, twelve astrological types, and twelve zodiac signs, may hold the key. Below, you will find a brief and accurate description of each zodiac sign's characteristics in love, for both men and women.

Men

ARIES

Aries men are not particularly deep or wise, but they make up for it in sincerity and loyalty. They are active, even aggressive lovers, but a hopeless romantic may be lurking just below the surface. Aries are often monogamous and chivalrous men, for whom there is only one woman (of course, in her absence, they can sleep around with no remorse). If the object of your affection is an Aries, be sure to give him a lot of sex, and remember that for an Aries, when it comes to sex, anything goes. Aries cannot stand women who are negative or disheveled. They need someone energetic, lively, and to feel exciting feelings of romance.

The best partner for an Aries is Cancer, Sagittarius, or Leo. Aquarius can also be a good match, but the relationship will be rather friendly in nature. Partnering with a Scorpio or Taurus will be difficult, but they can be stimulating lovers for an Aries. Virgos are good business contacts, but a poor match as lovers or spouses.

TAURUS

A typical Taurean man is warm, friendly, gentle, and passionate, even if he doesn't always show it. He is utterly captivated by the beauty of the female body, and can find inspiration in any woman. A Taurus has such excess physical and sexual prowess, that to him, sex is a way to relax and calm down. He is the most passionate and emotional lover of the Zodiac, but he expects his partner to take the initiative, and if she doesn't, he will easily find someone else. Taureans rarely divorce, and are true to the end – if not sexually, at least spiritually. They are secretive, keep their cards close, and may have secret lovers. If a Taurus does not feel a deep emotional connection with someone, he won't be shy to ask her friends for their number. He prefers a voluptuous figure over an athletic or skinny woman.

The best partners for a Taurus are Cancer, Virgo, Pisces, or Scorpio. Sagittarius can show a Taurus real delights in both body and spirit, but they are unlikely to make it down the aisle. They can have an interesting relationship with an Aquarius – these signs are very different, but sometimes can spend their lives together. They might initially feel attracted to an Aries, before rejecting her.

GEMINI

The typical Gemini man is easygoing and polite. He is calm, collected, and analytical. For a Gemini, passion is closely linked to intellect, to the point that they will try to find an explanation for their actions before carrying them out. But passion cannot be explained, which scares a Gemini, and they begin jumping from one extreme to the other. This is why you will find more bigamists among Geminis than any other sign of the Zodiac. Sometimes, Gemini men even have two families, or divorce and marry several times throughout the course of their lives. This may be because they simply can't let new and interesting experiences pass them by. A Gemini's wife or lover needs to be smart, quick, and always looking ahead. If she isn't, he will find a new object for his affection.

Aquarians, Libras, and Aries make good partners for a Gemini. A Sagittarius can be fascinating for him, but they will not marry before he reaches middle age, as both partners will be fickle while they are younger. A Gemini and Scorpio are likely to be a difficult match, and the Gemini will try to wriggle out of the Scorpio's tight embrace. A Taurus will be an exciting sex partner, but their partnership won't be for long, and the Taurus is often at fault.

CANCER

Cancers tend to be deep, emotional individuals, who are both sensitive and highly sexual. Their charm is almost mystical, and they know how to use it. Cancers may be the most promiscuous sign of the Zodiac, and open to absolutely anything in bed. Younger Cancers look for women who are more mature, as they are skilled lovers. As they age, they look for someone young enough to be their own daughter, and delight in taking on the role of a teacher. Cancers are devoted to building a family and an inviting home, but once they achieve that goal, they are likely to have a wandering eye. They will not seek moral justification, as they sincerely believe it is simply something everyone does. Their charm works in such a way that women are deeply convinced they are the most important love in a Cancer's life, and that circumstances are the only thing preventing them from being together. Remember that a Cancer man is a master manipulator, and will not be yours unless he is sure you have throngs of admirers. He loves feminine curves, and is turned on by exquisite fragrances. Cancers don't end things with old lovers, and often go back for a visit after a breakup. Another type of Cancer is rarer – a faithful friend, and up for anything in order to provide for his wife and children. He is patriotic and a responsible worker.

Scorpios, Pisces, and other Cancers are a good match. A Taurus can make for a lasting relationship, as both signs place great value on family and are able to get along with one another. A Sagittarius will result in fights and blowouts from the very beginning, followed by conflicts and breakups. The Sagittarius will suffer the most. Marriage to an Aries isn't off the table, but it won't last very long.

LEO

A typical Leo is handsome, proud, and vain, with a need to be the center of attention at all times. They often pretend to be virtuous, until they are able to actually master it. They crave flattery, and prefer women who comply and cater to them. Leos demand unconditional obedience, and constant approval. When a Leo is in love, he is fairly sexual, and capable of being devoted and faithful. Cheap love affairs are not his thing, and Leos are highly aware of how expensive it is to divorce. They make excellent fathers. A Leo's partner needs to look polished and well-dressed, and he will not tolerate either frumpiness or nerds.

Aries, Sagittarius, and Gemini make for good matches. Leos are often very beguiling to Libras; this is the most infamous astrological "master-slave" pairing. Leos are also inexplicably drawn to Pisces – this is the only sign capable of taming them. A Leo and Virgo will face a host of problems sooner or later, and they might be material in nature. The Virgo will attempt to conquer him, and if she does, a breakup is inevitable.

VIRGO

Virgo is a highly intellectual sign, who likes to take a step back and spend his time studying the big picture. But love inherently does not lend itself to analysis, and this can leave Virgos feeling perplexed. While Virgo is taking his time, studying the object of his affection, someone else will swoop in and take her away, leaving him bitterly disappointed. Perhaps for that reason, Virgos tend to marry late, but once they are married, they remain true, and hardly ever initiate divorce. In bed, they are modest and reserved, as they see sex as some sort of quirk of nature, designed solely for procreation. Most Virgos have a gifted sense of taste, hearing, and smell. They cannot tolerate pungent odors and can be squeamish; they believe their partners should always take pains to be very clean. Virgos usually hate over-the-top expressions of love, and are immune to sex as a mean s of control. Many Virgos are stingy and more appropriate as husbands than lovers. Male Virgos tend to be monogamous, though if they are unhappy or disappointed with their partner, they may begin to look for comfort elsewhere and often give in to drunkenness.

Taurus, Capricorn, and Scorpio make the best partners for a Virgo. They may feel inexplicable attraction for Aquarians. They will form friendships with Aries, but rarely will this couple make it down the aisle. With Leos, be careful – this sign is best as a lover, not a spouse.

LIBRA

Libra is a very complex, wishy-washy sign. They are constantly seeking perfection, which often leaves them in discord with the reality around them. Libra men are elegant and refined, and expect no less from their partner. Many Libras treat their partners like a beautiful work of art, and have trouble holding onto the object of their affection. They view love itself as a very abstract concept, and can get tired of the physical aspect of their relationship. They are much more drawn to intrigue and the chase- dreams, candlelit evenings, and other symbols of romance. A high percentage of Libra men are gay, and they view sex with other men as the more elite option. Even when Libras are unhappy in their marriages, they never divorce willingly. Their wives might leave them, however, or they might be taken away by a more decisive partner.

Aquarius and Gemini make the best matches for Libras. Libra can also easily control an independent Sagittarius, and can easily fall under the influence of a powerful and determined Leo, before putting all his strength and effort into breaking free. Relationships with Scorpios are difficult; they may become lovers, but will rarely marry.

SCORPIO

Though it is common to perceive Scorpios as incredibly sexual, they are, in fact, very unassuming, and never brag about their exploits. They will, however, be faithful and devoted to the right woman. The Scorpio man is taciturn, and you can't expect any tender words from him, but he will defend those he loves to the very end. Despite his outward control, Scorpio is very emotional; he needs and craves love, and is willing to fight for it. Scorpios are incredible lovers, and rather than leaving them tired, sex leaves them feeling energized. They are always sexy, even if they aren't particularly handsome. They are unconcerned with the ceremony of wooing you, and more focused on the act of love itself.

Expressive Cancers and gentle, amenable Pisces make the best partners. A Scorpio might also fall under the spell of a Virgo, who is adept at taking the lead. Sparks might fly between two Scorpios, or with a Taurus, who is perfect for a Scorpio in bed. Relationships with Libras, Sagittarians, and Aries are difficult.

SAGITTARIUS

Sagittarian men are lucky, curious, and gregarious. Younger Sagittarians are romantic, passionate, and burning with desire to experience every type of love. Sagittarius is a very idealistic sign, and in that search for perfection, they tend to flit from one partner to another, eventually forgetting what they were even looking for in the first place. A negative Sagittarius might have two or three relationships going on at once, assigning each partner a different day of the week. On the other hand, a positive Sagittarius will channel his powerful sexual energy into creativity, and take his career to new heights. Generally speaking, after multiple relationships and divorces, the Sagittarian man will conclude that his ideal marriage is one where his partner is willing to look the other way.

Aries and Leo make the best matches for a Sagittarius. He might fall under the spell of a Cancer, but would not be happy being married to her. Gemini can be very intriguing, but will only make for a happy marriage after middle age, when both partners are older and wiser. Younger Sagittarians often marry Aquarian women, but things quickly fall apart. Scorpios can make for an interesting relationship, but if the Sagittarius fails to comply, divorce is inevitable.

CAPRICORN

Practical, reserved Capricorn is one of the least sexual signs of the Zodiac. He views sex as an idle way to pass the time, and something he can live without, until he wants to start a family. He tends to marry late, and almost never divorces. Young Capricorns are prone to suppressing their sexual desires, and only discover them later in life, when they have already achieved everything a real man needs – a career and money. We'll be frank – Capricorn is not the best lover, but he can compensate by being caring, attentive, and showering you with valuable gifts. Ever cautious, Capricorn loves to schedule his sexual relationships, and this is something partners will just have to accept. Women should understand that Capricorn needs some help relaxing – perhaps with alcohol. They prefer inconspicuous, unassuming women, and run away from a fashion plate.

The best partners for a Capricorn are Virgo, Taurus, or Scorpio. Cancers might catch his attention, and if they marry, it is likely to be for life. Capricorn is able to easily dominate Pisces, and Pisces-Capricorn is a well-known "slave and master" combination. Relationships with Leos tend to be erratic, and they are unlikely to wed. Aries might make for a cozy family at first, but things will cool off quickly, and often, the marriage only lasts as long as Capricorn is unwilling to make a change in his life.

AQUARIUS

Aquarian men are mercurial, and often come off as peculiar, unusual, or aloof, and detached. Aquarians are turned on by anything novel or strange, and they are constantly looking for new and interesting people. They are stimulated by having a variety of sexual partners, but they consider this to simply be normal life, rather than sexually immoral. Aquarians are unique – they are more abstract than realistic, and can be cold and incomprehensible, even in close relationships. Once an Aquarius gets married, he will try to remain within the realm of decency, but often fails. An Aquarian's partners need uncommon patience, as nothing they do can restrain him. Occasionally, one might encounter another kind of Aquarius – a responsible, hard worker, and exemplary family man.

The best matches for an Aquarius are female fellow Aquarians, Libras, and Sagittarians. When Aquarius seeks out yet another affair, he is not choosy, and will be happy with anyone.

PISCES

Pisces is the most eccentric sign of the Zodiac. This is reflected in his romantic tendencies and sex life. Pisces men become very dependent on those with whom they have a close relationship. Paradoxically, they are simultaneously crafty and childlike when it comes to playing games, and they are easily deceived. As a double bodied sign, Pisces rarely marry just once, as they are very sexual, easily fall in love, and are constantly seeking their ideal. Pisces are very warm people, who love to take care of others and are inclined toward "slave-master" relationships, in which they are the submissive partner. But after catering to so many lovers, Pisces will remain elusive. They are impossible to figure out ahead of time – today, they might be declaring their love for you, but tomorrow, they may disappear – possibly forever! To a Pisces, love is a fantasy, illusion, and dream, and they might spend their whole lives in pursuit of it. Pisces who are unhappy in love are vulnerable to alcoholism or drug addiction.

Cancer and Scorpio make the best partners for a Pisces. He is also easily dominated by Capricorn and Libra, but in turn will conquer even a queen-like Leo. Often, they are fascinated by Geminis – if they marry, it will last a long time, but likely not forever. Relationships with Aries and Sagittarians are erratic, though initially, things can seem almost perfect.

Women

ARIES

Aries women are leaders. They are decisive, bold, and very protective. An Aries can take initiative and is not afraid to make the first move. Her ideal man is strong, and someone she can admire. But remember, at the slightest whiff of weakness, she will knock him off his pedestal. She does not like dull, whiny men, and thinks that there is always a way out of any situation. If she loves someone, she will be faithful. Aries women are too honest to try leading a double life. They are possessive, jealous, and not only will they not forgive those who are unfaithful, their revenge may be brutal; they know no limits. If you can handle an Aries, don't try to put her in a cage; it is best to give her a long leash. Periodically give her some space – then she will seek you out herself. She is sexual, and believe that anything goes in bed.

Her best partners are a Sagittarius or Leo. A Libra can make a good match after middle age, once both partners have grown wiser and settled down a bit. Gemini and Aquarius are only good partners during the initial phase, when everything is still new, but soon enough, they will lose interest in each other. Scorpios are good matches in bed, but only suitable as lovers.

TAURUS

Taurean women possess qualities that men often dream about, but rarely find in the flesh – they are soft, charming, practical, and reliable – they are very caring and will support their partner in every way. A Taurus is highly sexual, affectionate, and can show a man how to take pleasure to new heights. She is also strong and intense. If she is in love, she will be faithful. But when love fades away, she might find someone else on the side, though she will still fight to save her marriage, particularly if her husband earns good money. A Taurus will not tolerate a man who is disheveled or disorganized, and anyone dating her needs to always be on his toes. She will expect gifts, and likes being taken to expensive restaurants, concerts, and other events. If you argue, try to make the first peace offering, because a Taurus finds it very hard to do so – she might withdraw and ruminate for a long time. Never air your dirty laundry; solve all your problems one-on-one.

Scorpio, Virgo, Capricorn, and Cancer make the best matches. A relationship with an Aries or Sagittarius would be difficult. There is little attraction between a Taurus and a Leo, and initially Libras can make for a good partner in bed, but things will quickly cool off and fall apart. A Taurus and Aquarius make an interesting match – despite the difference in signs, their relationships are often lasting, and almost lifelong.

GEMINI

Gemini women are social butterflies, outgoing, and they easily make friends, and then break off the friendship, if people do not hold their interest. A Gemini falls in love hard, is very creative, and often fantasizes about the object of her affection. She is uninterested in sex without any attachment, loves to flirt, and, for the most part, is not particularly affectionate. She dreams of a partner who is her friend, lover, and a romantic, all at once. A Gemini has no use for a man who brings nothing to the table intellectually. That is a tall order, so Geminis often divorce and marry several times. Others simply marry later in life. Once you have begun a life together, do not try to keep her inside – she needs to travel, explore, socialize, attend events and go to the theater. She cannot tolerate possessive men, so avoid giving her the third degree, and remember that despite her flirtatious and social nature, she is, in fact, faithful – as long as you keep her interested and she is in love. Astrologists believe that Geminis do not know what they need until age 29 or 30, so it is best to hold off on marriage until then.

Leo and Libra make the best matches. A relationship with a Cancer is likely, though complex, and depends solely on the Cancer's affection. A Gemini and Sagittarius can have an interesting, dynamic relationship, but these are two restless signs, which might only manage to get together after ages 40-45, once they have had enough thrills out of life and learned to be patient. Relationships with a Capricorn are very difficult, and almost never happen. The honeymoon stage can be wonderful with a Scorpio, but each partner will eventually go their own way, before ending things. A Gemini and Pisces union can also be very interesting – they are drawn to each other, and can have a wonderful relationship, but after a while, the cracks start to show and things will fall apart. An Aquarius is also not a bad match, but they will have little sexual chemistry.

CANCER

Cancers can be divided into two opposing groups. The first includes a sweet and gentle creature who is willing to dedicate her life to her husband and children. She is endlessly devoted to her husband, especially if he makes a decent living and remains faithful. She views all men as potential husbands, which means it is dangerous to strike up a relationship with her if your intentions are not serious; she can be anxious and clingy, sensitive and prone to crying. It is better to break things to her gently, rather than directly spitting out the cold, hard truth. She wants a man who can be a provider, though she often earns well herself. She puts money away for a rainy day, and knows how to be thrifty, for the sake of others around her, rather than only for herself. She is an excellent cook and capable of building an inviting home for her loved ones. She is enthusiastic in bed, a wonderful wife, and a caring mother.

The second type of Cancer is neurotic, and capable of creating a living hell for those around her. She believes that the world is her enemy, and manages to constantly find new intrigue and machinations.

Another Cancer, Virgo, Taurus, Scorpio, and Pisces make the best matches. A Cancer can often fall in love with a Gemini, but eventually, things will grow complicated, as she will be exhausted by a Gemini's constant mood swings and cheating. A Cancer and Sagittarius will initially have passionate sex, but things will quickly cool off. A relationship with a Capricorn is a real possibility, but only later in life, as while they are young, they are likely to fight and argue constantly. Cancer can also have a relationship with an Aries, but this will not be easy.

LEO

Leos are usually beautiful or charming, and outwardly sexual. And yet, appearances can be deceiving – they are not actually that interested in sex. Leo women want to be the center of attention and men running after them boosts their self-esteem, but they are more interested in their career, creating something new, and success than sex. They often have high-powered careers and are proud of their own achievements. Their partners need to be strong; if a Leo feels a man is weak, she can carry him herself for a while- before leaving him. It is difficult for her to find a partner for life, as chivalrous knights are a dying breed, and she is not willing to compromise. If you are interested in a Leo, take the initiative, admire her, and remember that even a queen is still a woman. Timid men or tightwads need not apply. Leos like to help others, but they don't need a walking disaster in their life. If they are married and in love, they are usually faithful, and petty gossip isn't their thing. Leo women make excellent mothers, and are ready to give their lives to their children. Their negative traits include vanity and a willingness to lie, in order to make themselves look better.

Sagittarius, Aries, and Libra make the best matches. Leos can also have an interesting relationship with a Virgo, though both partners will weaken each other. Life with a Taurus will lead to endless arguments – both signs are very stubborn, and unwilling to give in. Leos and Pisces are another difficult pair, as she will have to learn to be submissive if she wants to keep him around. A relationship with a Capricorn will work if there is a common denominator, but they will have little sexual chemistry. Life with a Scorpio will be turbulent to say the least, and they will usually break up later in life.

VIRGO

Virgo women are practical, clever, and often duplicitous. Marrying one isn't for everyone. She is a neat freak to the point of annoying those around her. She is also an excellent cook, and strives to ensure her children receive the very best by teaching them everything, and preparing them for a bright future. She is also thrifty – she won't throw money around, and, in fact, won't even give it to her husband. She has no time for rude, macho strongmen, and is suspicious of spendthrifts. She will not be offended if you take her to a cozy and modest café rather than an elegant restaurant. Virgos are masters of intrigue, and manage to outperform every other sign of the Zodiac in this regard. Virgos love to criticize everyone and everything; to listen to them, the entire world is simply a disaster and wrong, and only she is the exception to this rule. Virgos are not believed to be particularly sexual, but there are different variations when it comes to this. Rarely, one finds an open-minded Virgo willing to try anything, and who does it all on a grand scale – but she is rather the exception to this general rule.

The best matches for a Virgo are Cancer, Taurus, and Capricorn. She also can get along well with a Scorpio, but will find conflict with Sagittarius. A Pisces will strike her interest, but they will rarely make it down the aisle. She is often attracted to an Aquarius, but they would drive each other up the wall were they to actually marry. An Aries forces Virgo to see another side of life, but here, she will have to learn to conform and adapt.

LIBRA

Female Libras tend to be beautiful, glamorous, or very charming. They are practical, tactical, rational, though they are adept at hiding these qualities behind their romantic and elegant appearance. Libras are drawn to marriage, and are good at imagining the kind of partner they need. They seek out strong, well-off men and are often more interested in someone's social status and bank account than feelings. The object of their affection needs to be dashing, and have a good reputation in society. Libras love expensive things, jewelry, and finery. If they are feeling down, a beautiful gift will instantly cheer them up. They will not tolerate scandal or conflict, and will spend all their energy trying to keep the peace, or at least the appearance thereof. They do not like to air their dirty laundry, and will only divorce in extreme circumstances. They are always convinced they are right and react to any objections as though they have been insulted. Most Libras are not particularly sexual, except those with Venus or the Moon in Scorpio.

Leos, Geminis, and Aquarians make good matches. Libra women are highly attracted to Aries men - this is a real case of opposites attract. They can get along with a Sagittarius, though he will find that Libras are too proper and calm. Capricorn, Pisces, and Cancer are all difficult matches. Things will begin tumultuously with a Taurus, before each partner goes his or her own way.

SCORPIO

Scorpio women may appear outwardly restrained, but there is much more bubbling below the surface. They are ambitious with high self-esteem, but often wear a mask of unpretentiousness. They are the true power behind the scenes, the one who holds the family together, but never talk about it. Scorpios are strong-willed, resilient, and natural survivors. Often, Scorpios are brutally honest, and expect the same out of those around them. They do not like having to conform, and attempt to get others to adapt to them, as they honestly believe everyone will be better off that way. They are incredibly intuitive, and not easily deceived. They have an excellent memory, and can quickly figure out which of your buttons to push. They are passionate in bed, and their temperament will not diminish with age. When she is sexually frustrated, a Scorpio will throw all of her energy into her career or her loved ones. She is proud, categorical, and "if you don't do it right, don't do it at all" is her motto. Scorpio cannot be fooled, and she will not forgive any cheating. Will she cheat herself? Yes! But it will not break up her family, and she will attempt to keep it a secret. Scorpios are usually attractive to men, even if they are not particularly beautiful. They keep a low profile, though they always figure out their partner, and give them some invisible sign. There is also another, selfish type of Scorpio, who will use others for as long as they need them, before unceremoniously casting them aside.

Taurus is a good match; they will have excellent sexual chemistry and understand each other. Scorpio and Gemini are drawn to each other, but are unlikely to stay together long enough to actually get married. Cancer can be a good partner as well, but Cancers are possessive, while Scorpios do not like others meddling in their affairs, though they can later resolve their arguments in bed. Scorpio and Leo are often found together, but their relationship can also be very complicated. Leos are animated and chipper, while Scorpios, who are much deeper and more stubborn, see Leos as not particularly serious or reliable. One good example of this is Bill (a Leo) and Hillary (a Scorpio) Clinton. Virgo can also make a good partner, but when Scorpio seemingly lacks emotions, he will look for them elsewhere. Relationships with Lira are strange and very rare. Scorpio sees Libra as too insecure, and Libra does not appreciate Scorpio's rigidity. Two Scorpios together make an excellent marriage! Sagittarius and Scorpio are unlikely to get together, as she will think he is shallow and rude. If they do manage to get married, Scorpio's drive and persistence is the only thing that will make the marriage last. Capricorn is also not a bad match, and while Scorpio finds Aquarius attractive, they will rarely get married, as they are simply speaking different languages! Things are alright with a Pisces, as both signs are emotional, and Pisces can let Scorpio take the lead when necessary.

SAGITTARIUS

Sagittarius women are usually charming, bubbly, energetic, and have the gift of gab. They are kind, sincere, and love people. They are also straightforward, fair, and very ambitious, occasionally to the point of irritating those around them. But telling them something is easier than not telling them, and they often manage to win over their enemies. Sagittarius tends to have excellent intuition, and she loves to both learn and teach others. She is a natural leader, and loves taking charge at work and at home. Many Sagittarian women have itchy feet, and prefer all kinds of travel to sitting at home. They are not particularly good housewives – to be frank, cooking and cleaning is simply not for them. Their loved ones must learn to adapt to them, but Sagittarians themselves hate any pressure. They are not easy for men to handle, as Sagittarians want to be in charge. Sagittarius falls in love easily, is very sexual and temperamental, and may marry multiple times. Despite outward appearances, Sagittarius is a very lonely sign. Even after she is married with children, she may continue living as if she were alone; you might say she marches to the beat of her own drum. Younger

Sagittarians can be reckless, but as they mature, they can be drawn to religion, philosophy, and the occult.

Aries and Leo make the best matches, as Sagittarius is able to bend to Leo's ways, or at least pretend to. Sagittarians often end up with Aquarians, but their marriages do not tend to be for the long haul. They are attracted to Geminis, but are unlikely to marry one until middle age, when both signs have settled down. Sagittarius and Cancer have incredible sexual chemistry, but an actual relationship between them would be tumultuous and difficult. Capricorn can make a good partner- as long as they are able to respect each other's quirks. Sagittarius rarely ends up with a Virgo, and while she may often meet Pisces, things are unlikely to go very far.

CAPRICORN

Capricorn women are conscientious, reliable, organized, and hard-working. Many believe that life means nothing but work, and live accordingly. They are practical, and not particularly drawn to parties or loud groups of people. But if someone useful will be there, they are sure to make an appearance. Capricorn women are stingy, but not as much as their male counterparts. They are critical of others, but think highly of themselves. Generally, they take a difficult path in life, but thanks to their dedication, perseverance, and willingness to push their own limits, they are able to forge their own path, and by 45 or 50, they can provide themselves with anything they could want. Capricorn women have the peculiarity of looking older than their peers when they are young, and younger than everyone else once they have matured. They are not particularly sexual, and tend to be faithful partners. They rarely divorce, and even will fight until the end, even for a failed marriage. Many Capricorns have a pessimistic outlook of life, and have a tendency to be depressed. They are rarely at the center of any social circle, but are excellent organizers. They have a very rigid view of life and love, and are not interested in a fling, as marriage is the end goal. As a wife, Capricorn is simultaneously difficult and reliable. She is difficult because of her strict nature and difficulty adapting. But she will also take on all the household duties, and her husband can relax, knowing his children are in good hands.

Taurus, Pisces, and Scorpio make good matches. Aries is difficult, once things cool off after the initial honeymoon. When a Capricorn meets another Capricorn, they will be each other's first and last love. Sagittarius isn't a bad match, but they don't always pass the test of time. Aquarius and Capricorn are a difficult match, and rarely found together. Things are too dull with a Virgo, and while Leo can be exciting at first, things will fall apart when he begins showing off. Libra and Aquarius are both difficult partners for Capricorn, and she is rarely found with either of them.

AQUARIUS

A female Aquarius is very different from her male counterparts. She is calm and keeps a cool head, but she is also affectionate and open. She values loyalty above all else, and is unlikely to recover from any infidelity, though she will only divorce if this becomes a chronic trend, and she has truly been stabbed in the back. She is not interested in her partner's money, but rather, his professional success. She is unobtrusive and trusting, and will refrain from listening in on her partner's phone conversations or hacking into his email. With rare exceptions, Aquarian women make terrible housewives. But they are excellent partners in life – they are faithful, never boring, and will not reject a man, even in the most difficult circumstances. Most Aquarians are highly intuitive, and can easily tell the truth from a lie. They themselves only lie in extreme situations, which call for a "white lie" in order to avoid hurting someone's feelings.

Aquarius gets along well with Aries, Gemini, and Libra. She can also have a good relationship with a Sagittarius. Taurus often makes a successful match, though they are emotionally very different; the same goes for Virgo. Aquarius and Scorpio, Capricorn, or Cancer is a difficult match. Pisces can make a good partner as well, as both signs complement each other. Any relationship with a Leo will be tumultuous, but lasting, as Leo is selfish, and Aquarius will therefore have to be very forgiving.

PISCES

Pisces women are very adaptable, musically inclined, and erotic. They possess an innate earthly wisdom, and a good business sense. Pisces often reinvent themselves; they can be emotional, soft, and obstinate, as well as sentimental, at times. Their behavioral changes can be explained by frequent ups and downs. Pisces is charming, caring, and her outward malleability is very attractive to men. She is capable of loving selflessly, as long as the man has something to love. Even if he doesn't, she will try and take care of him until the very end. Pisces' greatest fear is poverty. They are intuitive, vulnerable, and always try to avoid conflict. They love to embellish the truth, and sometimes alcohol helps with this. Rarely, one finds extremely unbalanced, neurotic and dishonest Pisces, who are capable of turning their loved ones' lives into a living Hell!

Taurus, Capricorn, Cancer, and Scorpio make the best matches. She will be greatly attracted to a Virgo, but a lasting relationship is only likely if both partners are highly spiritual. Any union with a Libra is likely to be difficult and full of conflict. Pisces finds Gemini attractive, and they may have a very lively relationship – for a while. Occasionally, Pisces ends up with a Sagittarius, but she will have to fade into the background and entirely submit to him. If she ends up with an Aquarius, expect strong emotional outbursts, and a marriage that revolves around the need to raise their children.

Tatiana Borsch

Made in the USA
Monee, IL
06 December 2021

84018036R10059